The *What You Need to Know . . .* books can get you up to speed on a core business subject fast. Whether it's for a new job, a new responsibility, or a meeting with someone you need to impress, these books will give you what you need to get by as someone who knows what they're talking about.

Each book contains:

- ▶ **What It's all About** – a summary of key points
- ▶ **Who You Need to Know** – the basics about the key players
- ▶ **Who Said It** – quotes from key figures
- ▶ **How You Need to Do It** – key steps to put your new-found knowledge into practice
- ▶ **What You Need to Read** – books and online resources for if you want to deepen your knowledge
- ▶ **If You Only Remember One Thing** – a one-liner of the most important information

You might also want to know:

- ▶ *What You Need to Know about Business*
- ▶ *What You Need to Know about Economics*
- ▶ *What You Need to Know about Project Management*
- ▶ *What You Need to Know about Leadership*
- ▶ *What You Need to Know about Strategy*
- ▶ *What You Need to Know about Marketing*

# WHAT YOU TO KNOW ABOUT

# STARTING A BUSINESS

KEVIN DUNCAN

CAPSTONE

*Library of Congress Cataloguing-in-Publication Data*

9780857082046(paperback), 9780857082053(epub),
9780857082060(emobi), ISBN 9781119979197 (ebk)

A catalogue record for this book is available from the British Library.

Set in 10.5/13.5 pt New Baskerville by Toppan Best-set Premedia Limited

Printed in Great Britain by TJ International Ltd., Padstow, Cornwall

For Sarah, Rosanna and Shaunagh.

# CONTENTS

| | |
|---|---|
| Introduction | 1 |
| 1 – The Idea | 7 |
| 2 – The Business Plan | 37 |
| 3 – Laws and Systems | 63 |
| 4 – The Money Bit | 81 |
| 5 – Sales and Marketing | 105 |
| 6 – People | 135 |
| 7 – Growth and Durability | 157 |
| 8 – Lifestyle Matters | 177 |
| Index | 205 |

# INTRODUCTION

Starting a business can be a daunting prospect, but it doesn't have to be as bad as some people make out. In fact, it's a hugely exciting time. Big plans can be inspiring, but doing the simple stuff well makes a huge difference. Some people try to overcomplicate matters, and this often leads to unnecessary delay, and can reduce confidence in the early days. This book takes a positive approach. Practical matters are kept straightforward, and there is plenty of advice on keeping in the right frame of mind. There is inspiration from people who have been there before, and plenty of back-up ideas for when things don't go quite as planned.

Millions of small businesses launch every year so you are not alone when it comes to thinking of starting one. Picking up this book is the first step on an adventurous and challenging road. From the beginning, the knack is to investigate the possible approaches for your business calmly and simply. Too many people flap around with hundreds of spreadsheets and lose their bearings in the process. So we'll take it gently so as to keep you saner in the crucial start-up phase.

In the early days, it is crucial to scrutinize the original idea very carefully. Of course, some are dead on arrival, and others need crafting before they make sense and can prove their value. Few are brilliant immediately, so you need patience and an open mind. Ideas are nothing if they cannot be enacted effectively, so we will be as clear as possible about this from the very beginning.

We will of course be examining the dreaded business plan. There is a skill to good business planning and anyone can learn it. Doing something is the first step. Too many businesses fail to get under way because they are still in the planning phase and never come out of it. It's a great feeling to discover that in fact you may be able to complete this in a matter of days.

Not surprisingly, there is always some boring stuff to cover, but when it's your own business somehow the motivation is that bit easier because you are the one to benefit. Knowing what you need to run an effective business is vital, and that means having a good working knowledge of the law, and appropriate systems to enable you to report business performance accurately.

The money bit may sound nasty but you can't run a business without it – it's actually what business is all about. So good budding entrepreneurs need to learn how to confront pricing, cash flow, supplier payment, and many other financial matters in a cheerful and pragmatic manner.

Nor can you run a business without some form of sales and marketing, so you need to let people know who you are, where you are, and what you do. You need to know where to find your customers, and how to communicate with them in a charming and positive way. People who start businesses often have a gift for this, but if it doesn't come naturally, don't worry, because there are simple things that anyone can do to promote their business.

You will soon discover that starting a business is a highly personal matter, and as such it is quite hard to take the emotion out of it. So in fact a lot of what at first appears to be factual ends up being emotional. The main reasons for this are that the original idea will be yours, pretty much all the decisions are yours, and the success of the venture is yours. So it is almost impossible to divorce the fortunes of the business from those of the owner, and that's you.

So it's all about you, which may seem rather scary at this stage, but in fact it turns out to be brilliant, because the rewards are all yours, and it's great to see a direct link between the effort you put in and the satisfaction you get back.

Each chapter has a number of common elements:

> **What It's All About** – A quick summary at the start listing the important points that will be covered.

> **Who You Need to Know** – Influential figures you need to know about.

> **Who Said It** – Quotes from famous figures to remind, inspire and amuse you.

> **What You Need to Read** – Suggestions of good sources for further reading at the end of each chapter.

> **If You Only Remember One Thing** – A short line or two summing up the contents of each chapter.

Starting a business is all about taking action. Careful thought and planning is vital of course, but there's no substitute for getting on and doing something. That is very much a theme of the book, and it is intentionally organized in such a way as to encourage you to get out there and do it.

# CHAPTER 1
# THE IDEA

## WHAT IT'S ALL ABOUT

► What *you* want to do
► Researching your market thoroughly
► Potential customers
► Whether it will make money
► Plans and execution

Starting a business is a matter of choice – no one can be forced into it. That's a very interesting thought, because so many people working in corporations don't have a great deal of choice. Suddenly then, you do. What would you like to do? It's a simple enough question, and yet can be extraordinarily hard to answer. It is a truly unique moment when you can decide something entirely by yourself. So it is worth taking proper care to get it right.

Copying something else is unlikely to be very fulfilling, unless of course that is a deliberate business strategy. More likely, you will have a view on how a product or service can be made or delivered in a better way, or in a manner that is specific to you. This needs to be looked at carefully before diving in. Clear the decks, create some proper thinking time, take a deep breath, and begin.

# IGNORE EVERYONE ELSE, WHAT DO *YOU* WANT TO DO?

People start businesses for hundreds of reasons. In the UK at any given time, about 4.5 million people are at it, out of a total labour market of about 30 million, so over one in six people don't need a corporation to earn a living.

The range of reasons for starting a business is vast and includes:

- I hated my boss
- Couldn't stand the politics
- Frustration with current job
- Got fired or made redundant
- I am, or I became, unemployable
- Convinced there must be a better way
- Wanted to be my own boss/have more control
- The chance to use my brain for my own benefit
- Run my life as I want
- Life changes everything
- Wanted to take a risk
- Always wanted to
- Wanted the challenge
- Wanted to create my own dream job
- Spotted an opportunity
- Had a safety net
- Wanted to make a lot of money
- A combination of fear and ambition

Work can be a frustrating business, as this list shows, and self-employment represents an alternative to enduring someone else's way of doing things. The original motivation doesn't matter that much. What matters very much is the manner in which you set about designing and enacting the business you wish to start.

The starting point is what you want to do. As far possible, this should be a pure thought, unencumbered by too many outside influences. So, your business is less likely to be a success if you start it for overly negative reasons that don't truly reflect your character. Bad ways to start a business include:

- ▶ Petulantly trying to prove a point
- ▶ Revenge against a former employee or rival
- ▶ Just in it for the money
- ▶ Wanting a short-term fix
- ▶ Deciding on a whim
- ▶ Diving into an idea you have not considered until very recently

In other words, knee-jerk reactions to your current circumstances don't work very well. It's okay to be spurred on by events, but it's not okay to jump into something without proper thought. So that means you need to ignore everyone else and work out what *you* want to do. The old advice from a mother to her daughter was to identify what you enjoy doing and then find someone to pay you to do it. This should be the basis on which you decide what type of business you wish to start. Once you have the essence of this, of course you will solicit opinion from others to sense check your thinking. But start on your own, and ask yourself what you really enjoy doing, and how you can make a living from that.

If this doesn't come naturally, try looking to your hobbies and passions, considering how they can be turned into a viable business idea, and defining who would pay for your knowledge or skill in that area. If you can generate an idea from this simple central thought, it will stand you in great stead later on. There are many reasons for this, but the most important are that it is easier to be a success when you enjoy what you do and it is less arduous working through tricky times when you instinctively like the subject matter that earns you a living.

# WHAT PRECISELY IS THE IDEA?

The original idea needs very careful scrutiny. Few are brilliant immediately. Ideas are nothing if they cannot be enacted effectively, so clarity of thought at the outset is absolutely vital. As Einstein once said, if you can't explain something to your grandmother, then you probably don't understand it properly yourself.

Something may be clear in your head, but what happens thereafter? Like Chinese whispers, everything can become distorted. The journey from your head to the wider world is a strange one. You need to have a vision of what your business could be, work out what you want to do, and find a way of explaining it clearly. Imagine you are going public and consider how you intend to let everyone else know. Your idea needs to follow this sequence:

▶ In your head
▶ Rough draft on paper
▶ Refined computer copy
▶ Explanation to someone who knows nothing about it

► Explanation to someone who knows something about it
► Refinement of the idea
► Acceptance or rejection of the idea

Pitching on a postcard is a good idea. If you can't explain in one sentence what the business will do (the 'elevator pitch'), then it's probably too complicated. Keep it simple. Don't let business speak affect your clear statement of the proposition. Some businesses are easy to describe, others not. If it's a well-known concept, then you may simply be saying 'It's a coffee shop'. No further explanation is needed, but it doesn't prove that it will be a success until we examine other factors, which we'll do in a minute.

# WHO SAID IT

"The only way to avoid making mistakes is to have no new ideas."
– Albert Einstein

If the business idea is not simple, then you still need to find the simplest language to describe it. Saying you work in IT solutions doesn't really explain anything. Don't get bogged down in the detail at this stage. 'It's an internet business that provides people with X' is fine for the moment. If you are having trouble, try explaining the customer benefit. This is the benefit that your customers derive from what you offer. It may well not be the same as what you do. How you deliver the product or service is rarely as interesting as the problem it solves. For example, in the case of a brand of biscuits, the manufacturer may claim they are 'lovingly hand-crafted from the finest ingredients', but the customer benefit is simply that they taste great.

If this simple expression of the idea meets with general acceptance, from you when you have lived with it for a while and from people you respect, then you should be able to move on. Importantly, though, if there are significant doubts then you may need to scrap it. There's nothing more boring than a person who insists on clinging onto a lame duck idea when it patently isn't going to work. Bear in mind that most successful businesses have rejected many prototypes and initial thoughts. It's a crucial editing skill that you need to adopt when starting a business. So, be precise about the idea, ditch all the bad ones, and refine the expression of it so that it is short, clear, and intelligible for anyone.

# WHO YOU NEED TO KNOW
## *Seth Godin*

Seth Godin is one of the world's most prolific writers and bloggers – something of a web legend with a cult following. His main talent as a writer is to impart technical zeal without the baggage of geek jargon. He holds an MBA from Stanford University and has been called the Ultimate Entrepreneur for the Information Age by *Business Week* magazine.

As a well-respected speaker, marketing guru and agent of change, he has stacks of advice for businesses large and small. In his book *Purple Cow* he encourages businesses to offer something that is remarkably different from any other product – do the opposite of everyone else and you will be more distinctive.

He wants ordinary people like us to start a movement. Stop 'sheepwalking' your way through work and start doing fresh and exciting work, he says. We can all create a remarkable future by running ingenious businesses. With the advent of the internet, practically anyone can do it. You just need faith, a good idea, and plenty of energy to enact it.

His general theme is all about personal empowerment, which is spot on for those starting a business. In his book *Linchpin*, for example, he explains that you may well be indispensable, and shows how to drive your career and create a remarkable future. With more than ten short, very readable books out, and a significant blog, it's easy to soak up some of his inspiration.

# WHAT EXACTLY WILL YOUR BUSINESS BE?

This looks like the same question as 'What precisely is the idea?', but it isn't. We now move on to describing what the business will do in order to fulfill the idea. You need to define a number of important parameters to work out how successful it could be. Ask yourself these questions:

▶ *What category will the business operate in?*
This may not be as easy at it sounds. Starbucks could variously be described as a purveyor of coffee, a sandwich bar, an internet café, and so on. Work out which market you are operating in.

▶ *Is it a product or a service?*
A product is sourced or manufactured and sold at a certain price. A service may have a life long after the initial purchase. Many businesses provide both.

▶ *Does it offer multiple products or services?*
Offering one thing is straightforward. A range is more complicated and requires careful designing.

▶ *What does it cost to provide or produce these?*
If the cost of sourcing or production is too high, then your margin will prove insufficient.

▶ *What price will you sell them at?*
Some companies can work well on low prices if they have high volume. Others rely on lower frequency of sale and higher margin. Work out which area your business will operate in.

▶ *Is that proposed margin realistic?*
If the base price of an item or service is too well-known, there will be a limit to the mark-up that customers will tolerate.

▶ *Is it sufficient for what you need?*
If you need more than the market can stand, then the idea may be flawed, or be incapable of delivering what you want.

▶ *What is the projected income?*
This forces you to provide an initial feel for how much business you will generate.

▶ *And the projected profit?*
This highlights the difference between having plenty of income, but no profit. There is little point in this. As the old saying goes, turnover is vanity, profit is sanity.

Your answers may at this stage be vague or unknown, but you have to start somewhere. If they are numerical, don't exaggerate them. This will lead to problems later. Bear in mind that most businesses don't achieve what was expected in the first year, and most are slower at getting off the ground than the owners would like, so always round figures down without being too pessimistic. If the answers are factual, then keep them straight. If you don't know the answer, then go and find out. This might lead to an explanation of your business along the following lines. Let's look at a London plumbing business:

▶ *What category will the business operate in?*
Rosie's Plumbers is the first all-female plumbing business. It operates in the home plumbing market in the London area.

▶ *Is it a product or a service?*
Both. The largest part of the business will be services paid for by the hour, and 20% of income will come from mark-up on parts.

▶ *Does it offer multiple products or services?*
Yes. It fixes all domestic plumbing needs.

▶ *What does it cost to provide or produce these?*
Anticipated costs are $x$, with a proposed salary for one plumber of $y$.

▶ *What price will you sell them at?*
£80 per hour, with an anticipated 20 hours booked per week.

▶ *Is that proposed margin realistic?*
Yes. 80% of income will be derived from services paid for by the hour. 20% of income will come from parts marked-up at 20%.

▶ *Is it sufficient for what you need?*
Yes/no.

▶ *What is the projected income?*
Income in year one is projected at £1,600 a week, £6,400 a month and £70,400 in an eleven-month year.

▶ *And the projected profit?*
20% will yield profit of over £14,000, and any mark-up on parts will be a bonus.

We won't do the full plan just yet, but you can immediately see that precise thinking leads to a clear statement. This in turn leads to an accurate plan and a clear understanding of the maths involved. Of course, you might go through this exercise and discover that the business is far too generic and so will not survive or make sufficient inroads into the competition in your area. Or you may find that the sums don't work, leaving you either with too little income or an outright loss. These are vital discoveries. Don't get depressed about it. Throw out dreadful plans, and think harder about half-baked ones until they look as though they will be a success.

# RESEARCH YOUR MARKET THOROUGHLY

It's not wise to dive in and start a business without doing some proper research. You might have a hunch that a certain idea will be a success, but there may well be a lot that you don't know. Information is power, and it enables you to make better, less random, decisions. Research your market thoroughly by asking these sorts of questions:

> ▶ If your business is going to operate in a specific area, will the market support it? For example, if you plan to open a restaurant, how many already exist, what type of service do they offer, and what are their prices like?
> ▶ How do you plan to position your business – up-market, mid-market, or down-market?
> ▶ Will the area support another business such as yours or is the market already saturated?
> ▶ What kind of people will buy your product?

> ► Can you reach all of your customers through affordable communication channels?
> ► Are there different buying circumstances, such as planned, impulse or special occasion?

This type of information shouldn't be hard to come by. If you are planning a local business, then get out and about. Walk the streets. Get on the bus or the train. Get in the car. Work out journey times, catchment areas, and the presence of similar businesses. Obviously, if you are planning to start a fish and chip shop and there are already three in the same street, you need to have an extremely good reason or an extraordinary angle to justify going ahead.

If you are planning an internet business, bear in mind that geography could be irrelevant. Instead your research could all be online, comparing similar services and product offerings, looking at speed of delivery and pricing as more likely indicators of competitiveness. If lots of other businesses can provide what you are proposing for a similar price and just as fast, then you may need to think again.

If you discover lots of businesses that offer the same as your idea, don't panic straight away. Bear in mind that tiny alterations to the detail can still make your idea viable. For example, moving a location 1000 yards can make all the difference. So can altering the price by a few percent. Or reducing the rent. Or increasing product quality or brand image. Or speed of delivery. Or bulk delivery. Or the presence or absence of one member of staff. Keep analyzing these elements until the proposition and the maths slot into place. Equally, if your research overwhelmingly demonstrates that your idea is not going to be a success, then face facts and ditch it for a better one.

# DO CUSTOMERS REALLY NEED YOU?

As with so many start-up questions, this one seems so simple, but it is extraordinary how many businesses launch without answering this satisfactorily. Think it through. Most markets are now oversupplied, so customers can get pretty much anything they want, from anywhere. Competition is fierce. It might be local. Or your most significant competitor could be in China or India, and capable of delivering just as fast. And possibly cheaper. Or with higher quality.

Against this backdrop, you really do need to ask: do customers really need you? If you can't answer with a convincing 'yes', then you may not have a viable business. We will examine the appeal of your proposition in the next chapter, but at this stage you need at the very least the inklings of some reason that supports an affirmative answer. It may only be a small point of differentiation, but it must be there. It will most likely come from an area such as unique product or service, better quality, more competitive price, speed of delivery, convenience, reliability, or even being more pleasant to deal with.

If you have very little to claim in any of these areas, then there may well be no customer need. If that's true, then you should not start your business. There must be some relationship between the appeal of what you offer and potential customer demand. If you cannot identify this link, then you are unlikely to have much success. If that's an obvious flaw straight away, then don't waste time. Change the idea and think of something better. If it's unclear one way or the other, then probe deeper with questions like these:

- ▶ What kind of people will buy your product?
- ▶ What sort of age, social class, sex, or disposable income defines them?
- ▶ What will your best customers tend to have in common?
- ▶ Do your potential customers fall into different groups?
- ▶ What other types of products and services do they buy?
- ▶ How many of them are there?
- ▶ What is a realistic frequency of purchase for your product or service?
- ▶ How often will you communicate with your existing customers?
- ▶ How will you attract new ones?

Here you begin to develop a pen picture of your ideal customer. There may be many different types, or an ideal profile that perfectly fits what you have in mind. Once you have defined this, you can match the profile with the number of people in your catchment area or online community that fit the description. Match this to your pricing and frequency of purchase, and you begin to get a feel for income and profit.

# WILL YOUR BUSINESS MAKE MONEY?

We will produce a plan in the next chapter, but it is important that you begin to develop a knack for working out whether your idea is likely to make money from the outset. All good small business owners develop this skill early on. It prevents you from making poor decisions, stops you fooling yourself about likely success, and is invaluable when you introduce new ideas post-launch. Here are some money-related points to consider:

> ▶ *Concentrate on the money, but don't become obsessed with it*
> Wandering round with a spreadsheet all day won't get the business under way. If the idea is sound then the money will follow. Don't just go for cash as an objective – it will prove unsatisfactory in the long run.
> ▶ *Weigh up the Service v. Product distinction*
> Are you offering a service, a product, or both? It is important to look at the distinction between the two. A product is tangible. A service involves interaction that often goes beyond the moment of purchase. As we saw in the plumber example,

a combination is acceptable so long as you know what percentage is coming from each.

► *Work out how to have a high margin*
Can you offer something that relies purely on your skill or experience? If so, you may be able to keep your costs down to near zero. This gives you great flexibility in pricing, and the amount of time you spend working per year.

► *Try to sell what you do, not materials with a mark up*
Products have price points that are easier for the customer to guess. Services can be priceless. Even the most inexperienced customer has a rough working knowledge of what something should cost. They will understand you have to make a mark-up, but there will be an upper limit that could hinder your profitability.

► *The price–quality equation: If you cost a lot, you must be good*
People like paying for high quality goods and services. Don't sell yourself cheap. Most people starting a business undervalue what they do. This is a mistake. Think carefully about your true value and make your prices match that.

► *Aim for 50% repeat business within 3 years*
It costs a lot less to gain repeat business than to start from scratch, so you should aspire to the high standards that generate it. 50% is of course an arbitrary figure, but try to design something that encourages repeat purchase. This will save you reinventing your business every year, and all the cost and effort that goes with it.

▶ *Don't be small-minded about money*
Speculate and you will accumulate. Invest upfront, within reason. Be generous and put something in before you expect something back. Treat your customers well and pay your bills on time. Develop a reputation for generosity and fair dealing.

▶ *Be canny about requests for free or 'win only' work*
If you spend your first year behaving like a charity, then you'll go bust. It's okay to provide a judicious amount of trial product or service as a taster for what you offer, but only to a certain level. Then you need to be paid. So set your level and remember to draw the line.

▶ *Consider flexible pricing*
If you achieve a certain (non-discounted) price for something, then consider charging more next time. This point is specifically for service businesses. Start with a fair price and review it periodically to see if your market can tolerate higher prices based on the quality of what you provide.

# GREAT PLANS ARE NOTHING WITH POOR EXECUTION

It's the oldest trap in the book. Someone has a great idea but strangely nothing happens. How many times have you stood in the pub with someone claiming that they

# WHO YOU NEED TO KNOW
*James Dyson*

In the late 1970s James Dyson, having become frustrated with his Hoover's diminishing performance, had the idea of using cyclonic separation to create a vacuum cleaner that would not lose suction as it picked up dirt. Similar to much entrepreneurial lateral thinking, the idea of the cyclones came from the spray-finishing room's air filter in his factory. Partly supported by his art teacher wife's salary, and after five years and many prototypes, Dyson launched the G-Force cleaner in 1983. However, no one would launch his product in the UK as it would disturb the valuable cleaner-bag market, so he launched it in Japan through catalogue sales. Manufactured in bright pink, the G-Force had a selling price of the equivalent of £2,000. It won the 1991 International Design Fair prize in Japan.

Still none of the major manufacturers would take it, so in June 1993 he set up his own manufacturing company and research centre in Malmesbury, Wiltshire. The product now outsells those of some of the companies that rejected his idea and has become one of the most popular brands in the United Kingdom. By 2005 Dyson cleaners had become the market leaders in the United States by value.

Dyson's story is a classic: a bright idea followed by years of dedication in the face of rejection from all the powers that be. His fortune is now estimated at £1.1 billion.

have a great idea? Three years later they are saying the same thing, and nothing has happened. Inertia is arguably the biggest problem for any start-up. Someone has a great idea. They tell everyone they are planning something. They write lots of things down. They do a lot of preparatory work. They visit the bank and get a lot of planning templates. They fill out a large number of spreadsheets. And so the list of pre-work goes on. Nine months later, the business still hasn't launched and they haven't earned a bean.

All the great artists will say that an idea is nothing without execution. A great idea remains just that until it has been enacted. When someone stares at a painting and says 'I could have done that', the point is that they didn't. Someone else did. In their book, *Execution*, Bossidy and Charan point out that people mistakenly think of execution as the tactical side of the business, which seduces leaders and business owners into concentrating on the so-called bigger issues. This creates a gap between the promises leaders make and the results the company actually delivers. In 2000, 40 of the top Fortune 200 company CEOs were removed for that very reason. Someone who says they have ten priorities doesn't know what they are talking about. We don't think our way into a new way of acting, we act our way into a new way of thinking.

So you need to keep a close eye on the planning element of your start-up phase. Consider these points:

- ▶ Before you start the planning phase, work out how long it should realistically take
- ▶ You can extend this amount of time, but not by too long
- ▶ Stick rigidly to review periods: where have I got to?
- ▶ Fix regular reviews with a respected friend to keep on track
- ▶ Choose a launch date for your business and try to stick to it
- ▶ If you are still stuck in the planning phase, analyze why

▶ Make it an objective to get out of the planning phase as fast as possible

▶ Quantify the cost of not launching your business

As you can see, all of this effectively adds up to a rap sheet of penalties. If you haven't launched, then you won't have any income, which may mean that you can't pay the bills. As we shall see in the next chapter, planning is effectively a good thing, but not too much of it. There's no substitute for getting on with something. Your philosophy should be to give it your best shot and fix it as you go along.

# THE BEGINNINGS OF SELF-BELIEF

To create real change, you have to become it. We now need to get out of the planning phase and into the '*No, I really am doing it*' phase – not so much a phase as a new, and quite possibly permanent, way of life. This is a crucial leap of faith. Here are some irritating excuses for not getting things done.

> '*The planning phase will be completed in Quarter Four.*'

> '*We'll go live when beta testing has ironed out any bugs in the system.*'

> '*We're still in a pre-test scenario.*'

You may well recognize this sort of phraseology from the corporate world. All it means is that it isn't happening at the moment. If it isn't happening, then it doesn't exist. If it doesn't exist, then no one can buy it. And if no one is buying it, then you haven't got any income. It's all pretty straightforward really. Put another way, the quickest way to get money is to generate some business.

Self-belief can be retarded by fear. The most commonly cited things about starting that worry people is a long list which includes cash flow, giving up a big salary, making the leap, personal isolation, not being able to generate leads, uncertainty, not having the confidence to hire other people, delay between work and being paid, having a really slow start, or not even knowing where to start.

At some point, most people suffer from a lack of self-belief, uncertainty, and a worry that they lack the specialist expertise. Self-belief is an essential prerequisite of anyone starting a business, even if you have to face your demons in private. If you don't believe in yourself, then why should any potential customer? Take the time to work out what you are all about. You don't have to be motivated like some missionary zealot on daytime American television, just a positive person who is keen to get things done. If you suffer from doubts, try to get them out of your system in your spare time. Part of the key to this may well be making sure that you take sufficient time off and spend time on your hobbies to provide a relaxing counterpoint to the stress of work.

Uncertainty is completely natural, and possibly even desirable. There is a school of thought that says that anyone confronted with a daunting task, such as playing a musical instrument live in front of 50,000 people or playing in a cup final at Wembley, performs better if they are slightly nervous. Those who are too laid-back can often be outperformed by those who are more on top of their game. So you probably should be slightly apprehensive. Uncertainty is endemic in business start-ups – you can't predict for sure how it will go. But what you can do is have a 100% bearing on your approach to it.

Lack of specialist expertise can be rectified by having a candid think about what you can't do, and finding out who can. Technical experts such as lawyers, accountants, Information Technology specialists, bookkeepers and so on, can all be tracked down and engaged to do the things that you can't. There is also a massive element of learn-as-you-go-along when you run your own business – that's part of the fun.

## WHO SAID IT

"Every revolutionary idea evokes three stages of reaction:

1. it's completely impossible
2. it's possible but it's not worth doing
3. I said it was a good idea all along."

– Arthur C. Clarke

# TEST-DRIVING YOUR IDEA

As soon as you can, it's a good idea to test-drive your idea. By this time you will certainly have written it down, been through several redrafts, looked at the numbers, and explained it to anyone who will listen. However, all of that remains theoretical, and doesn't completely prove or disprove whether your business idea has long-term merit.

This is when you need to invent a way of testing what you have come up with, in a way that limits the damage as much as possible. The internet provides a brilliant new way of doing this, effectively for free. In the same way that it could help you to research your market in the first place, it can provide a forum for testing whether it will work in reality. You may know the old joke about academics: it works in practice, but does it work in theory? Here we want to know whether it is going to work in practice, but without going to the expense of setting everything up before we know. Try this online:

> ▶ Identify a community who you believe will be interested in your product or service
> ▶ Find them online
> ▶ Explain your business proposition in the simplest terms possible
> ▶ Include everything that enables them to comment, such as pricing, delivery time, and so on

- ▶ Design a short questionnaire
- ▶ Ask whether they would buy your product or service
- ▶ If necessary, offer an incentive to make them reply
- ▶ Choose a sample size that is large enough to be representative
- ▶ If your business idea allows it, consider offering a trial of your product or service

Analyze the results and make changes based on what you discover. If your business idea is physical, such as setting up a shop, then try to replicate the circumstances of early trading but without going to the full expense. So, instead of renting premises, hiring staff, and getting involved in all the normal start-up costs, set up a stall somewhere and try selling what you can for some trial days. Ask for comment. Experiment with pricing and use what you find as a test market.

So, to sweep up the themes of this chapter, start by thinking very carefully about what you want to do, and take the time to articulate precisely what the idea is. Then do some methodical research and test your idea on others to gauge customer reaction. Sketch out an initial shape, and test-drive it in a way that gives you a feel for its validity without exposing yourself to heavy expense or too much delay. If the response is disappointing, then face facts and make some changes before trying again.

# WHAT YOU NEED TO READ

▶ Dave Stewart and Mark Simmons's *The Business Playground* (Prentice Hall) does a great job of helping to bring your idea to life. Use the exercises to express your idea in an original way.

▶ *Whatever You Think, Think The Opposite* (Penguin) by Paul Arden can be read in about ten minutes, and is full of great little ideas.

▶ The National Federation of Enterprise Agencies – *www.nfea.com* – explains how businesses can get started, and provides independent and impartial advice, training and mentoring to new and emerging businesses.

▶ *Purple Cow* (Penguin) by Seth Godin is short and inspirational. You can read it in an hour or two and brace yourself for some brave decisions about your business idea, and an honest assessment of whether it is truly going to work.

▶ UK Intellectual Property Office – *www.ipo. gov.uk* – gives advice on how to define and protect your idea if it is unique, and can help you get the right type of protection for your creation or invention.

▶ If you have become bogged down, Matt Kingdon's *Sticky Wisdom* (Capstone Publishing) includes a range of techniques for thinking more creatively and moving you on to to something more productive.

# IF YOU ONLY REMEMBER ONE THING

Take the time to make sure that your business idea really suits you, and that it will be very appealing to potential customers.

# CHAPTER 2

# THE BUSINESS PLAN

## WHAT IT'S ALL ABOUT ➡

- ▶ The proposition
- ▶ A simple, realistic plan
- ▶ How much money you need
- ▶ Name, identity and branding

A lot of people get really hung up on the business plan. They worry hugely about it because they may never have done one. The most important thing that anyone starting a business needs to understand is that the plan does not have to be complicated. Some highly successful businesses have been launched with the simplest of plans. There is a significant difference between the plan that is required by you as opposed to one that is required by another party, such as a bank or investor. The less someone else knows about your idea, the more they will need written down. The more money they are putting in, the more reassurance they will need. But all business plans should have some basic components: the proposition, the money requirement, the working environment, the company name, and the support elements. There is a knack to good business planning. Doing something is the first step. Too many businesses fail to get under way because they are still in the planning phase and never come out of it.

# WHAT'S THE PROPOSITION?

The proposition is what you are offering as a business. It is essential that you become adept at describing what you do. Propositions vary hugely, from basic descriptions (*'I am a florist'*) to complicated technical stuff (*'We have the most advanced software platform in the call centre market, outperforming the ZX22 by a staggering 43%.'*) Sole traders and those starting businesses will always want to be at the simpler end of this spectrum, because if you can't explain to a stranger what you do in thirty seconds, then it is most likely that you haven't got a clear business proposition.

Deciding on your proposition does not have to be complicated. In the same way that there are only a limited number of strategies in the world, there are only a limited number of propositions. Consider what yours might be and work through some possibilities. A clear proposition can come from many places, and will vary hugely by market. The important thing is that it is easy to understand and directly relevant to your potential customers. To help you articulate these ideas, here are some examples based on a hypothetical business that sells apples:

- ▶ Price: Adam's Apples are the cheapest/best value in town
- ▶ Results: Adam's Apples win more awards than any other
- ▶ Reliability: Adam's Apples are perfect every time
- ▶ Guarantee: If you aren't happy with Adam's Apples we'll give you your money back
- ▶ Exclusivity/specific market/niche: Adam's Apples have been awarded the Royal Family's seal of approval
- ▶ Service: We will deliver Adam's Apples anywhere in the country
- ▶ Quality: Adam's Apples have been voted the best in the country

► Uniqueness/innovation: Only Adam's Apples come from prize-winning orchards
► Originality: Adam's Apples were the first ever to be sold in the UK
► Experience: Adam's Apples has 500 years of growing experience
► Image: Adam's Apples are eaten by the famous film star Johnny Starr

Have a think about which characteristics are most appropriate for your market. Write it down as a complete sentence, and then read it out loud. If it sounds daft, then change it. When you have a version you are happy with, try it out on your partner, or your mum. They may say it is incomprehensible, in which case you will need to try again.

# WHO SAID IT

"If you think you're too small to make an impact, try going to bed with a mosquito."
– **Anita Roddick**

# THE ONE-PAGE BUSINESS PLAN

The one-page business plan enables anyone who has been labouring for some time over massive forms and spreadsheets to simplify matters. This simple plan should unclog it all, and should not take more than twenty minutes to complete. You will need to be able to fill in the numbers to establish whether your business is likely to work or not.

Step 1: How much do I want to earn each year?

_____

Step 2: A realistic expenditure per customer/visit/ transaction/project is:

_____

Step 3: A realistic number of customers/visits/ transactions/projects is:

_____ per day
_____ per week
_____ per month
_____ per year

Step 4: How much money will this frequency generate?

£_____ per day
£_____ per week
£_____ per month
£_____ per year

Step 5: Now deduct all costs from the £ per year figure:

Per year total: £_____

Minus costs: £_____

Remaining: £_____

(If your salary is included in these costs, then make sure it equals the figure in Step 1. If it doesn't, see Step 6.)

Step 6: The figure remaining should equal or exceed the figure in Step 1. If it doesn't, change something. This could be:

Expenditure per customer

Number of customers

Costs

The amount you want to earn each year (if you were very ambitious)

All of the above

**Step 1**: Start by writing in the figure you want to earn. Many of you will be thinking: how can I decide what I will earn when I haven't done the plan yet? That's exactly the point. Most business plans are unhelpful precisely *because* they build an income or profit figure from a set of hypothetical variables. That doesn't help you to work out whether your business will sustain you or deliver the income you want. It's simple, but effective. That's why it is instructive to start at the end. So write down what you want to earn. This can either be the total profit at the end of the year that will go straight into your pocket as the owner of the business, or a decent salary paid for by the business. The net effect will be the same.

**Step 2**: Now you need to take a stab at a realistic cost per customer, visit, transaction, project, or whatever the appropriate description is for the business that you intend to start. Let's take a couple of examples. If you want to run a coffee shop, then you might put in £5 per visit. If you think your customers will only buy one cup of coffee, then it might be just £1. If you think they will stay for breakfast, then it might be £5. If you are selling to a corporate market where visitors come in for hours on end and work on their laptops, then it might be £10. Or, if your business is installing boilers for central heating systems, then the price might be £2,000 per installation with a £250 mark-up on each sale. The point is that no one would be selling boilers at the same frequency or price as cups of coffee, so work out the parameters that apply to your market and choose an appropriate average price per transaction.

**Step 3**: The number of customers/visits/ transactions/projects will vary depending on the nature of your proposed business. The simplest way to do the calculation is to break it down into tiny units, and then build it back up again. Look at it by day, then multiply it by the number of days in a week, month or year that you will be trading. In the case of a coffee shop, the business might sell 20 cups of coffee per hour in an 8-hour day. Assuming a 5-day week, allowing 4 weeks a month, and one month off for holiday, the maths looks like this:

160 per day (assuming 20 per hour, and an 8-hour day)
800 per week (assuming 5 days a week)
3,200 per month
35,200 per year (assuming one month off for holiday)

You can see how every variable is critical. If your pricing is wrong, then so is the whole model. If you open for an extra day per week, or hour per day, what happens to the figure?

**Step 4**: Once you have completed Step 3, it is a simple matter to multiply your figures by the price per customer, visit, or transaction that you settled on in Step 2. In this example, it is:

£800 per day (assuming £5 per visit)
£4,000 per week
£16,000 per month
£176,000 per year (assuming one month off for holiday)

This last 'per year' figure is the big one you have been waiting for.

**Step 5**: This total income figure is not profit. It is what the business takes in, not you personally. Now you have to work out what your costs will be. There are two basic ways of doing this:

1. Subtract from the expenditure per transaction every element of cost needed to fulfill that transaction. What's left is the margin. If there is nothing left, then your pricing is wrong or the business plan is fundamentally flawed. For example, if you have a 20% margin on every coffee shop transaction, then for each one £4 is cost and £1 is margin.

2. Alternatively, look at the entire business over the whole year. Add up everything you will need to pay for. Now subtract that figure from the 'per year' figure in Step 4.

**Step 6**: The figure remaining should equal or exceed the figure in Step 1. If it exceeds it, then you may well have a successful business model. If there is a ridiculously massive profit, then check your assumptions and figures again to be certain. If it doesn't equal or exceed your expectation, then don't panic yet, but you will have to change something. This could be:

▶ Expenditure per customer
▶ Number of customers
▶ Costs

▶ The amount you want to earn each year

▶ Any combination, or all of the above

This seems a simple list, but it includes a huge number of variables and assumptions, so take your time. You may find that you have incomplete information so you can't be sure of a certain figure. If so, go and find out otherwise you will be starting your business under false pretences. Keep going and rework the plan frequently. If, after many attempts, the plan never generates the surplus that you want, then you may have to conclude that the proposed business isn't going to work.

# WHO YOU NEED TO KNOW
### *Jeff Bezos*

After graduating from Princeton in 1986, Jeff Bezos worked on Wall Street in computer science before becoming a vice-president at Bankers Trust. He founded Amazon.com in 1994 after making a cross-country drive from New York to Seattle, writing up the Amazon business plan on the way. If nothing else, this proves how quickly a clear and successful business plan can be written.

After setting up the original company in his garage, Amazon eventually led him to become one of the most prominent dot-com entrepreneurs and a billionaire. Bezos is known for his attention to business process details. As described by Condé Nast's *Portfolio.com*, he 'is at once a happy-go-lucky mogul and a notorious micromanager . . . an executive who wants to know about everything from contract minutiae to how he is quoted in all Amazon press releases.'

The elements of the Amazon business model can provide great inspiration for any business plan, as they are a textbook case of thinking differently. Cutting out the middleman, aggregating millions of sellers, and creating software that gives its customers suggestions for more purchases make it one of the most successful businesses of all time. But it doesn't stop there. Amazon is constantly reworking its business plan and functionality to reflect new market opportunities and changing circumstances.

# HOW MUCH MONEY DO YOU NEED?

This sounds obvious, but many would-be business owners don't really cover the groundwork in this area. What is required here is not a forest of spreadsheets – just a really clear impression of how your business will work financially. Put simply, there are three types of money that you will need to examine:

1. Investment at the start
2. Monthly cash flow
3. The profit (monthly or annual)

Here is the layperson's guide to the three types.

## 1. Initial investment

Looking first at the investment needed at the start:

▶ Do you need to put any money in at all at the beginning? Pause on this one for a moment. If the answer is no, then don't do it.

▶ If you do need to borrow from some other source, what demands will the lenders make on getting it back? Banks want interest. Investors want cash back. They don't lend money out of kindness, and they may want to be involved in the way you run the business. Therefore, if you can do it without them, then do.

▶ If you have to put money in yourself, when are you going to get it back? Don't delude yourself by excluding this amount from your assessment of whether the business is going to be a success.

Many people who have recently started a business say that their business is 'successful' whilst simultaneously failing to remember that the business owes them thousands. This may be acceptable in the early stages, but not if there is no likelihood of you being repaid in the foreseeable future.

## 2. Monthly cash flow

This is the amount of income you need each month. Write down what you need. Then write down what you think you can get. Then build in time delays for late payment in the early days. This becomes your first cash-flow projection. This projection has to be very, very realistic. You must have a reasonable level of confidence that it is achievable. You need to distinguish carefully between income and profit. Never be tempted to call income profit. You can have a huge amount of income and yet still be making a loss. Make sure that you make proper allowance for all the outgoings that may crop up, as well as an amount to pay yourself as salary to keep the wolf from the door.

Calculate how much you need to make each month. Once you write it down, it is more likely to happen. (This is a general principle that works for almost everything.) You can have a sensible minimum and maximum, but it is better if you have just one figure. Now you have to work out where it's coming from. Write down a realistic list of the value of your income in the first three months. If this turns out to be too fanciful, write a more realistic list next time. As you become better at predicting, you will naturally build in time lags to reflect slow decision-making and slow payment.

## 3. The profit

The final thing to consider is the profit margin. Ask yourself:

- ► How much is the profit?
- ► Does it vary depending on what you have sold?
- ► Does it vary by month or season?
- ► Does it fluctuate wildly?
- ► Why?
- ► What would make it more consistent?
- ► What would make it higher?
- ► What are the tolerance levels?
- ► What is the average target?
- ► Is that realistic?
- ► Is it good enough for you?

You need to keep a regular and close eye on this. You also need to decide whether you wish to draw on the profit margin monthly, annually or over any other time period. If you need the profit margin monthly, does this mean that your business plan does not include an amount for your own salary? If so, is that wise or realistic? If you can take the profit annually, how are you keeping tabs on the surplus that is (hopefully) building up? Can you equate it back to the running monthly amount?

Be aware that if you manage to convince yourself that you can wait quite a long time to realize a certain margin (a year or more), then you may well have a vulnerable business. Successful businesses make a good margin with almost everything they do, effectively from day one. Consider this carefully. There is no point in driving yourself into the ground all year only to make a few percent, unless you are extremely happy with the figure that it generates.

## GET YOUR WORKING ENVIRONMENT RIGHT

Your business plan needs to take into account the type of working environment that is most likely to prove a success. Given that running your own business is a daily process of motivation and reinvention, you cannot hope to achieve this if you don't like where you work. Some businesses require a place of work away from home. If this is the case for yours, then do consider:

▶ Does the place that I work in really reflect my style?

> ► Is my journey to work sensible or is it just as bad as travelling to a salaried job in a company?
> ► Do I get to fraternize with like-minded people, or would I be better off somewhere else?

It is important that you think about the mood and style in your work place, for both you and any staff or colleagues. Match the environment you choose, and the way you fit it out, to the nature of your business and the mood you want to create for your customers.

If you plan to work at home, there are all sorts of things that you can do to get comfortable. Some people like to have a clearly differentiated room to work in where they can spread out, have all their stuff, and generally make a mess. Others only need a desk in the corner of the bedroom. Work out your preferred style. Decide on the level of tidiness you require about the place and arrange things accordingly. If you have a partner or other family members around you at home, talk to them about the bits that matter to you. What is out of bounds? Which things do you use in a working context that are in the house? Are there any aspects of other people's clutter and behaviour that prevent you from getting things done? If so, have you found a polite way of discussing it? Once you have mentioned it, they can understand better that the home is also a working environment, and perhaps make a few adjustments to help.

One way or another, you need to be inspired to get your work done: if your environment isn't right, change it.

These questions apply also to your chosen work environment if you intend to run a company with staff, or with regular interaction with customers. Assuming the money allows it, plan for a workplace that reflects your style and has a reasonable chance of keeping you and your staff sane and happy. You may need to start modestly, but if you are choosing offices, try to make sure that there is plenty of natural light, somewhere nearby to take a break, and a reasonable journey to work. If you are choosing a shop, try to make the premises reflect the product you are intending to sell.

Financially, aim to keep a sensible balance between cutting corners and overstretching. It may be appropriate to invest upfront in premises before your income is known, as long as you have thought carefully about the likelihood of getting a return on your investment. If this is doubtful, consider starting somewhere more modest and then moving when cash allows. On the other hand, if your business concept relies heavily on location or the feel of the environment, then weigh up carefully whether compromising on this could jeopardize the initial success of your business.

# PROGRESS NOT PERFECTION

When forging your business plan, do consider that the rough shape will do. This may sound like heresy in as much as many would claim that everything has to be perfect before you proceed to launch. However, the pursuit of perfection is precisely what prevents many businesses from ever getting going. This is because perfection never quite arrives. Too many businesses sit around pontificating about the so-called 'perfect' solution that is just around the corner. The trouble is, around the corner is where it usually stays. Many Japanese companies practice *Kaizen* (the art of continual improvement), but none of them ever claim they have it perfect.

So aim for progress, not perfection. Another way of stopping your plan being paralyzed by the possibility of 'just another thing' is to pursue MAYA: Most advanced yet acceptable. This approach encourages a business idea to be pushed as far as it can, but stops short of neutering itself by refusing to proceed unless everything is perfect. This may sound like a cop out, but it isn't. If you genuinely think you can find perfection, then hats off to you. More likely, though, you will be tempted to use the possibility of it as an excuse not to proceed, and that's no help to you at this critical early stage when the important thing is forward motion. Give it your best shot and fix things as you go along.

Let's consider some examples. On the money front, keep your calculations simple. Stick to round figures such as hundreds and thousands, rather than getting bogged down in the fine maths. Always err on the side of caution so that you have natural slack built in to your calculations. When it comes to timing, bear in mind that everything will probably be delayed, so draft your first plan, and then push it all back by two or three months to produce a more realistic projection. When it comes to product description, get it down in a sentence or two and then move on. Don't be distracted at this stage by fine detail such as design, legal copy, and so on. As long as you know how it can be enacted, then that is enough at this stage.

## WHO SAID IT

"The first step to getting what you want out of life is this: decide what you want."
– Ben Stein

## INVEST IN A DISTINCTIVE NAME AND IDENTITY

Your plan should allow for a distinctive name and identity. Your business needs to look good. Your company, shop or service needs a memorable name, a good logo, high quality headed paper, good quality signage, and business cards that invoke a reaction. Every detail counts. Don't skimp on quality of paper or thickness of business cards. Thin business cards are as weak as a limp hand-shake. Don't have them printed at a booth in a railway station. Check the spelling and punctuation really carefully on everything you produce. What many businesses fail to realize is that if there are mistakes in the way the business markets itself, many potential customers will conclude that what they offer will be as shoddy as their marketing materials.

Choosing a name for your business can fraught, but it can be approached methodically. There are five main types of company name:

1. Descriptive (Premier Sandwiches)
2. Owner-named (Dave's Sandwiches)
3. Multiple owner-named (Johnson Hobson Wilson Potato Peeler)
4. Pointless initials (DS Ltd)
5. Irrelevant but memorable (Orange, as in the mobile phone company)

If you wish to portray a solid but unremarkable image, then the descriptive approach may be justified. It is worth noting, however, that inventive branding has permeated almost every product category these days, so you should be as brave as you can be. The second option may be relevant if you have a reputation from a past life and it will be helpful for past clients to know that it's your business. In the case of Dave's Sandwiches, this is unlikely, but if you are a prominent expert in a specific field, then it may be relevant.

Multiple owner-named company names are unwieldy and hard to remember. As a start-up this is unlikely to be an issue, but if you are going into business with several partners then do consider the pitfalls of choosing a long-winded name just to satisfy the egos of the founding partners. It may not benefit the business, so resist this route if you possibly can, because it usually just leads to hoots of derision from potential customers.

Option four, pointless initials, is also highly undesirable. A quick glance at the phone book reveals thousands and thousands of these acronyms. Initials say nothing about you and are unremarkable, so try to resist using them. The last option, irrelevant but memorable, can be fun if it is done well. For example, if you work in a fairly dry sector, the use of a fun, lively name might make your business more memorable. All of this is of course a matter of personal taste, but usually it really is worth dreaming up a distinctive, memorable name for your business, and working out how much time and money needs to be allowed for in the plan in order to enact it.

# GET THE HELP YOU NEED

It may be the case that you simply cannot complete your business plan without help, or that you already know you will not be able to run your proposed business without it. Either way, it is important to work out exactly what that outside help might be. First of all, let's look at

# WHO YOU NEED TO KNOW
## *Tom Peters*

Tom is the doyen of business gurus, having written the classic *In Search of Excellence* in the 1980s with his partner, Robert Waterman. He has been variously described as the uber-guru of business and the father of the post-modern corporation. He originally identified the basic principles of how to run a successful business and stay ahead of the competition. These included a bias for action (get out there and try something), stay close to the customer (don't be distracted by the internal stuff) and hands-on, value-driven (top companies make meaning, not just money) – all of which is food for thought when starting a business.

He regularly writes a blog, espousing his view that it's the soft things that matter, although he admits they are very hard to do. Hundreds of small acts of humanity add up to big improvements in operational effectiveness. Big plans don't work – small steps get things done. Serious play beats serious planning – all practical ideas evolve from prototypes. *Do it, fix it, try it* should be the mantra of successful companies. It is worth comparing his classic approach with that of some of the internet entrepreneurs.

the help you may need to compose the plan. If you are uncertain what needs to go into the plan, there are many books on the subject, and the websites at the end of this chapter should point the way. Help with the financial elements can be provided by most high street banks, which have ready-made templates of what they want to see in a business plan. Ask your bank for theirs and use the format if necessary.

Researching your market and looking at the competition is usually something you could and should do yourself. If this is not possible or appropriate in your area, then investigate market surveys and research panels that can be purchased. The data can often add significant rigour to a plan. If it is a new market, consider commissioning an online survey to save time and money. If you need to show your plan to others but it lacks pazzazz with regard to presentation, then consider downloading images and data from the web, or using design software to liven it up with graphics, illustrations and projections. This is not to propose a smoke and mirrors approach to the plan, but to give it a lift if others need to be convinced of its value before launch.

There may be a case for involving other people in the design of the plan. If the financial projections are genuinely complicated, and necessarily so, then you may need to ask an accountant or other money expert to help create, or perhaps just check, the figures. If the legal issues are complicated, then seek specialist advice. If there are areas of experience that you lack, then ask for advice from those who have been there before.

When it comes to who should be involved when the business does actually launch, make sure you consider who these people should be when you write the plan. Some may be kind enough to offer their services for free, but others will need paying, and so their costs should be built into your projections from the beginning. The overriding rule is that if you don't know how to do something yourself then find someone who does. This applies equally to the creation of the business plan and the running of the business once it is under way.

A clear proposition lies at the heart of a good business plan, as does clarity and brevity of expression. You should be able to explain your plan on a postcard, or at the very most one page. Work through the investment, the working environment and the name, and admit if you need outside help. Put it all together, and you are close to starting out.

## WHAT YOU NEED TO READ

▶ Fried and Hansson's *Rework* (Vermilion) encourages you to view everything back to front, which may help to unclog your plan if it is looking dull, predictable, or unexciting, particularly to a potential investor.

▶ *The Little Big Things* by Tom Peters (Harper Collins) is a lively canter through 163 ways to pursue excellence in business, which will undoubtedly push your standards higher when reviewing your proposition and product offering.

▶ Jack Trout's *In Search of the Obvious* (John Wiley and Sons Ltd) is an inspiring re-dedication to keeping things simple. Use it if your plan has become too complicated.

▶ There are several websites that can help with what needs to be considered in a business plan. *www.smallbusiness.co.uk* has lots of advice for start-up companies, guides and tips on starting a business, raising finance, business grants and loans, and managing staff.

▶ *www.businessballs.com* has advice on how to write a business plan and free templates that you can download and fill in.

# IF YOU ONLY REMEMBER ONE THING

Too many businesses fail because they never come out of the planning phase. Doing something is the first step.

# CHAPTER 3
# LAWS AND SYSTEMS

## WHAT IT'S ALL ABOUT

- ▶ Legal requirements
- ▶ Getting the accounts right
- ▶ Setting up systems and technology
- ▶ Insurance

It might sound a bit dry, but being well organized is vital when you are starting a business. Even the most flamboyant and bohemian artist needs to send out invoices, pay the bills and stay the right side of the taxman – not very glamorous perhaps, but very necessary. Before you raise your eyebrows to the heavens and turn over the page, do consider one vital point: most of the tedium of administration can be offset by doing it once properly at the beginning. Thousands of businesses have wasted huge amounts of time trying to fix something they didn't set up properly in the first place, so it's worth taking the time to get it right first time.

It is very difficult to generalize about systems because they are highly specific to the type of business you are setting up. Broadly speaking, you will need to make sure that everything your company does is legal, that you get paid properly for what you do, pay the right tax, and have accounts that are appropriately organized. You will then need systems that ensure you can keep track of all this.

# LEGAL REQUIREMENTS

Knowing what you need to run an effective business is vital. Start as you mean to go on with a good working knowledge of the law, and appropriate systems to enable you to report business performance accurately. At the very beginning, you need to decide whether you will be a sole trader or a limited company. A sole trader can be 'Tom Jones trading as Tom's Garage' and does not require any particular registration other than a bank account that is clearly separate from his personal bank account. This is a necessity to ensure that money moving from one to the other is correctly monitored for tax purposes. It also helps you know where you stand. Sole trader status effectively allows the individual to get on and earn a living with the minimum of fuss and administration. It is a perfectly viable employment status for anyone who has an uncomplicated business with little in the way of staff, employees, or any other elements that make life more complicated.

A limited company doesn't have to be as grand as it sounds. As a rough guide, anyone expecting to earn over £50,000 a year should look at the possibility. Although there is a slight correlation between a business being larger and the benefits of being a limited company, it is not the only consideration. It is more likely to be beneficial if you want the kudos of being limited, if you can see tax efficiency as a result, and if you are happy to have your report and accounts available for anyone to examine at Companies House. Smaller businesses that do not want the hassle of two tax returns and who value their privacy highly may prefer to be sole traders. Anyone can register a company at Companies House for a small fee, and there can be as little as just one director and employee – in other words, just you. As the director, you are responsible for filing the report and accounts each year, and for paying both corporation tax and your personal tax.

Although this involves two types of tax, it can actually work out as a lower grand total if your trading circumstances are suitable.

There are of course lots of different types of company. Community Interest Companies (CICs), for example, are limited companies with special additional features, created for people who want to conduct a business for community benefit, and not purely for private advantage. This is achieved by a 'community interest test' and an 'asset lock', which ensure that the CIC truly is established for community purposes and the assets and profits are dedicated to those purposes. Registration of a company as a CIC has to be approved by the regulator who also has a monitoring and enforcement role. That's a pretty special case, as is Limited Liability Partnership, in which business partners protect themselves against personal loss whilst at the same time trading together. If you are unsure, ask your accountant about the differences between the types, and whether any apply to you.

Tax laws change over time, but typically corporation tax will be less than half that of the higher rate personal tax band, such as 20% versus 40%. This means that if the sole owner of a limited company runs legitimate costs through the business and doesn't take out too much money at any one time, having a limited company could be beneficial. Owners can take their money out of the business in two ways. They can pay themselves a dividend at any time, or they can put themselves on the payroll, in which case all the normal rules applicable to an employee of a corporation will apply, such as National Insurance. We will cover this more in the next chapter.

As well as financial matters, there may be legal requirements with regard to how the business conducts itself and interacts with the public. Sandwich shops and coffee shops will be subject to food standards and need to ensure they adhere to all the necessary requirements. Those businesses open to the public will need to meet all appropriate Health and Safety standards required by law, and be aware of the need for disabled facilities, fire regulations, security, and so on. If the business you plan to start is subject to any of these, then you need to find out what all the legal requirements are and prepare for them. This preparation includes knowing what is needed, finding out the associated costs, and building those into the business plan.

For service businesses – a very broad category that could include anything from advice and consultancy to design and anything remotely creative – another important legal area is that of intellectual property (IP). This is the fraught area of having a stock in trade based on ideas that your business generates. How do you mitigate against the possibility of your ideas being copied? It's a difficult business. Clearly, if a tangible product is taken without permission or payment, then it is illegal and identifiable as theft. This is harder to prove with ideas. So if the business you plan to start will be dealing in such an area, it is important to look at any mechanisms that can protect your work. Patents may be applied for to cover new product ideas. IP may be asserted if you register your work in advance in suitable places – your website, your bank, with a trade association, on your terms of business – that can prove your ownership of them. The law of the land stretches to almost every corner of a business. The list of requirements naturally lengthens the more complex, large and interactive your business is. Online resources explaining all these laws and what they mean are at the end of this chapter.

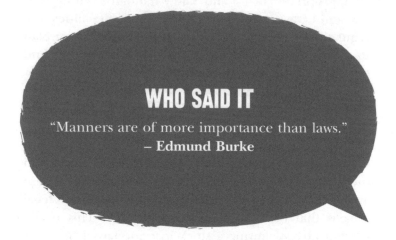

## WHO SAID IT

"Manners are of more importance than laws."
– **Edmund Burke**

# GETTING THE ACCOUNTS RIGHT

Setting up a good accounting system is crucial for lots of reasons. First, as the owner of the business you need to know the true state of your finances at any given moment so that you can make sensible decisions. Second, it is paramount that you know if you are working hard but not being paid on time, or at all. Third, you need to know if you are making a profit for all your effort. Fourth, you need a good working knowledge of what tax obligations and other major bills are coming up. Fifth, the accounts will be the first thing that any prospective purchaser of your business in the future asks for, so they need to be in good order. And sixth, you must keep it all legal.

The list is probably longer but the message is clear: you need well-organized accounts to run a good business. So they need to be set up properly when you start out. The best way to do this is to employ an accountant. They can advise you on how to establish your financial systems, and in all probability they will have their own that you can use. This is by far the best approach, but if you cannot afford an accountant or you decide not to engage one, then at the very least you must have a decent bookkeeping system. Again, you can employ a bookkeeper who will arrange and record everything for you, but if you choose not to you can buy or download software to set your system up. Putting all your financial information into such software is not complicated, but it does require discipline on your part. It's no use having brilliant software and then stuffing all your expense receipts in a drawer somewhere and hoping everything will be all right. You need to discipline yourself to log all your financial transactions in a methodical way. This means setting aside a certain time once a week, or month, or whatever frequency suits the nature of your business. Alternatively, design or buy a computer system that does all this for you electronically. One way or another, make sure it is all right up to date to avoid nasty surprises.

To summarize the basics of what you will need to ensure your accounts are in order, at a bare minimum you will need a system that accurately records:

- ▶ All outgoing expenditure: costs, salaries and expenses
- ▶ All income
- ▶ All tax due and paid (including VAT if relevant)
- ▶ How much cash there is in the business
- ▶ All costs due to be paid soon
- ▶ Any debtors, what they owe and how long they are overdue

Without becoming obsessed with the minutiae, as the owner of the business you should have a good working knowledge of all these figures at any given moment during the year. Should you fail to do this, there may be financial surprises lurking that could surface when you are least expecting it.

# SETTING UP SYSTEMS AND TECHNOLOGY

Money systems are vital, but there is so much more to getting your business organized, and much of it is not financial. Consider for example information technology (IT). There are thousands of different systems to choose from, and between them they can probably solve almost any problem you may have, or provide an organizational

# WHO YOU NEED TO KNOW
### *Michael E. Gerber*

Michael E. Gerber is often described as the world's number one small business guru. His book, *The E Myth Revisited*, sold more than one million copies, and is based on the home truths that every successful entrepreneur has learned by experience. Businesses typically move from entrepreneurial infancy through adolescent growing pains to the mature perspective, and the biggest mistake they can make is to work *in* the business rather than *on* it.

He is the founder of a company called E-Myth Worldwide, based in California, and author of several books, as well as being a highly sought-after speaker and small business revolutionary.

His crucial observation is that the adolescent phase of the business is where most of the trouble starts. This is where early consideration of legal requirements and decent systems will stand a business in good stead. Getting some help to weather this period could be vital, and all the better if the owner of the business has anticipated this likely need to avoid a short-term crisis with a nasty deadline.

## WHO SAID IT

"Legal obligations have escape clauses; moral obligations do not."
– John A Marshall

format to suit your business. Don't just dive in and pick the first one you come across, or one that's free. Take the time to work out what your needs are, and then find IT that fits the bill. This will effectively become your IT strategy. Ask yourself these types of questions:

- ▶ Which aspects of my business could benefit from IT?
- ▶ How many systems do I need?
- ▶ Can all my needs be handled by one system?
- ▶ What would happen if I needed to change the system in the future?
- ▶ How do I prevent failure or collapse of any vital functions?
- ▶ What back-up facilities do I need?
- ▶ How much can I justify paying for an IT system?

Naturally, the fewer systems you have, the better. You may need software for a wide range of needs such as stock keeping, supplier management, sales ledger, customer database, accounting, prospecting, and so on. If you plan to run a high frequency but low margin business such as a sandwich shop, then you will need detailed customer transaction information, but may require less knowledge of your customers. In other words, you need to know exactly how much you are selling of what, but not so much to whom. For higher margin but lower frequency businesses, such as clothes shops, travel agents, hotels and garages, longer-term customer records will be vital so that you can stay in touch, prompt further sales and market to your customer base at the appropriate frequency.

Customer Relationship Management (CRM) is the modern phrase that encompasses all this. The idea is to have a comprehensive system for building a decent customer base, ensuring that you look after them properly in the future, and marketing your products and services to them at suitable intervals. We will look at this in greater detail in Chapter 5, but for the moment consider the scale of what this might involve and whether a suitable IT system could help. The most obvious example in which a software system could be of use is where you anticipate that your business will be involved in hundreds or thousands of transactions. Clearly no single individual could keep track of them all, so that's where you need a system to do it for you.

Also bear in mind that the same principles apply to your suppliers and any partners or colleagues you may have. If you are expecting to have a large number of suppliers, you will need to have all their details in one place, with a clear method for renewing stock, logging invoices and payments, receiving orders, and generally keeping on top of everything. It's also good to review your relationship with them from time to time to make sure both parties are happy, and getting what they want from the arrangement. If you plan to have a business partner, or staff, then you need to work out how you are going to keep them informed. With one or two people this may not be an issue, but as soon as the numbers rise, you will need a system of some kind. Many collaboration tools can be bought online. These can cover everything from file sharing systems and coordinated diary management to free telephony and online conferencing facilities. Work out the best method of keeping people informed and in touch, and set up a system to facilitate it.

## WHO YOU NEED TO KNOW
### *Michael Dell*

While a student at the University of Texas, Michael Dell started an informal business upgrading computers at home. He applied for a vendor license to bid for contracts for the State of Texas, and won them by not having the overheads of a computer store.

In January 1984, he banked on his conviction that the potential cost savings of a manufacturer selling PCs directly to customers had enormous advantages over the conventional indirect retail channel, and registered his company as 'PCs Limited'. Operating out of a condominium, the business initially sold around $80,000 in upgraded PCs, kits, and add-on components. After relocating to a business centre, he employed some order takers, a few more people to fulfill them, and a manufacturing staff (in his own words) 'consisting of three guys with screwdrivers sitting at six-foot tables'. The venture's capitalization cost was just $1,000.

In 1992 at the age of 27, Dell became the youngest CEO to have his company ranked in *Fortune* magazine's list of the top 500 corporations. By 1996, he started selling computers over the web, and launched the company's first servers. Dell soon reported $1 million in sales per day from dell.com, and in the first quarter of 2001 reached a world market share of 12.8 percent, passing Compaq to become the world's largest PC maker. The company's combined shipments of desktops, notebooks and servers grew 34 percent worldwide and 30 percent in the United States at a time when competitor's sales were shrinking.

Dell bucked pretty much every system previously set up in the computer industry whilst setting up a new one of his own: stripping out all the overhead, and dealing direct with customers to provide them with customized products.

# INSURANCE

There is almost no limit to the different types of insurance that you might need for your business, and your needs will differ wildly depending on the nature of it. Starting with the simplest possible set-up, consider the sole trader working from home. At base level, you may not legally require any insurance at all, but this may not be a wise approach. Bricks and mortar insurance is a legal requirement, and so your home should be insured already, but do consider whether any aspect of your proposed business will change that. For example, do you intend to make any alterations to accommodate your new business? Most homes have contents insurance, but not all. If any aspect of your new life means changes in this area, then change your insurance. This could be as simple as taking out extra cover for your new computer, printer and hard-drive back up, or more complex if you plan to store any stock at home. If so, what is the cost to you of losing any or all of it?

Then consider yourself. What happens if you cannot work for a significant period such as more than a couple of weeks? If this would be severely detrimental to the business, then you will need some form of key man insurance. For a monthly payment, this will pay out an agreed annual amount if you are incapacitated mentally or physically. If the new business is to become the cornerstone of your livelihood, or that of any dependents, then you may also want to investigate health insurance and life insurance. On the pure financial front, you might also want to consider loss of income insurance to cover book debts, and the additional expenses of a VAT or tax inspection. They all cost and may never be required, but it is as well to consider them all in your new life.

As soon as you propose to run a business from specific premises other than your home, a whole new complicated world opens up. Having offices or any place of work where the public have access means you are liable for much more. Consider some of the following:

- ▶ employers liability – a legal requirement if you have staff
- ▶ public liability – if something happens in your work place
- ▶ product liability – if something happens with a product you provide
- ▶ product insurance – protecting items such as stock and equipment against fire, theft and malicious damage
- ▶ vehicle insurance – cars, vans, fleets, and anything else automotive

This is not an exhaustive list. Your bank manager can advise on insurance products to cover most of these in detail. Make sure that you consider every aspect of how your proposed business will interact with the world, and what all the implications are for insurance. Don't depress yourself, but do create a disaster planning scenario in which you envisage everything that could possibly go wrong, and then make provision for it as best as you can. Even if you cannot afford to insure all of it at the beginning, make a note to review your needs after a year to see if you want to upgrade or introduce more cover as cash flow improves.

Finding out about the law is a vital part of starting a business. Any shortcuts taken at this stage are likely to rebound nastily later in the life of your company. So do make sure that you fully understand your obligations and take the necessary steps to build the costs into your plan, and take the right action. The same goes for setting up suitable systems. Careful thought at the beginning about the right way in which to organize your accounts and purchase the most suitable technology will stand you in good stead later on.

## WHAT YOU NEED TO READ

▶ All the health and safety legislation in the UK is explained at *www.hse.gov.uk/legislation*. This tells you what you need to consider and how to go about it.

▶ The only online resource you really need for all matters relating to legislation, tax, VAT and pretty much every aspect of what is important financially when starting a business is *www.hmrc.gov.uk*, the site of HM Revenue and Customs.

► *The E Myth Revisited* is an excellent book to read on the systems and approaches you might need when starting a business, and could save a lot of errors later on. There is also a lot of material on *www.e-myth.com*.

# IF YOU ONLY REMEMBER ONE THING

Have a good working knowledge of the law, and create appropriate systems to help you to really understand how your business is performing.

# CHAPTER 4

# THE MONEY BIT

## WHAT IT'S ALL ABOUT

- ▶ Dealing with your bank
- ▶ Securing finance
- ▶ Tax and pay
- ▶ How to have a decent margin
- ▶ Looking ahead to avoid a crisis

As we saw in the last chapter, legal matters and systems have a strong link to the financial elements of your business, and it is of course important that you set everything up correctly and keep them in order as time goes by. But there is another aspect to money, and that is your attitude to it. Almost every case study concerning business success stories says the same thing: businesses established purely to make cash rarely do so. Those with a strong sense of purpose and integrity fare better, and the money flows from those principles. Cash is not an end in its own right.

# CONCENTRATE ON THE MONEY

From now on, when you discuss money, it will be not in some abstract way based on a remote budget that was agreed by someone you have never met. It will be a highly personal matter. When you are starting a business, it will be your own money. It has been said that you don't really appreciate what running your own business means until you have experienced a bad debt, so it is essential that you become comfortable talking about money straight away. If you don't, you will probably agree to provide unspecified amounts of work or goods over unclear time periods, and in some instances you might not get paid. Alternatively, you may consistently sell products at margins so low that your business will not be viable. Although this sounds obvious, huge numbers of business-people pursue a large volume of sales so that they can marvel at the scale of their operation. They may well be proud of their turnover, but frequently they are barely making a profit. There is no merit in rushing around all year generating things to do and creating the impression of success when you aren't actually making money.

Keep on top of what the money is doing, but don't obsess over it. Companies do not simply generate money by concentrating on it. They ensure that the business is working properly, and if they are delivering excellent products and services then it is likely that the numbers will take care of themselves. Work out a rough numerical shape of what the business requires, and then get on with implementing the activity that will make it happen. It is important to have a feel for figures without getting bogged down in the minutiae. This skill does of course improve with experience, but it can be acquired more quickly by sketching the overall shape from the outset and then mapping performance against that shape over time. Designing a business with certain products and prices, and then seeing what frequency of purchase will yield a certain monthly sales figure is one way of doing it. But it may not yield the figure you want, so many entrepreneurs prefer to set a figure as a target and shoot for that. Not surprisingly, this 'finger in the air' figure is always larger than the scientifically generated figure, but it has the virtue of giving you and your staff and colleagues something more aspirational to aim for.

This shape, albeit very loosely based on mathematics, becomes the template for all operations in the first year of trading. If it is well communicated and understood by partners and colleagues, then running the business becomes significantly easier because everyone knows what they are aiming for, and so pulls in the same direction. If this is left to chance, or not explained at all, then the sales figures for the business are likely to arrive in a much more haphazard fashion.

## WHO SAID IT

"The two most beautiful words in the English language are cheque enclosed."
– **Dorothy Parker**

# DEALING WITH YOUR BANK

At the heart of any good financial system is your relationship with your bank. From the beginning, it is important to explain to them what you are planning to do, and what resources you will need. Make sure that you become familiar with all the methods by which you can move money around and stay in touch with your finances. As well as a conventional branch relationship, have a look at telephone banking, internet banking, text alerts and all the electronic versions of possible transactions. Automate as much as possible to save time and the possibility of something being overlooked.

First, consider the nature of the different bank accounts you will need. In a limited company this may be only one, accompanied by a clear bookkeeping system that shows the money coming in and going out. In a complex business, however, several may be needed to deal with different products, services, and subsidiary companies. Talk this through carefully with your bank. Second, you need to establish a very clear distinction between your personal money and that of the business. This is essential to keep everything above board, and provide a crystal clear picture of your income, the company's income, any tax due on either, and the true financial state at any moment. Third, you may require an account for gaining interest on cash held, for setting aside allowances for future accounts (such as a large tax bill), or as a war chest for future plans for the business. Many current accounts, for example, generate no interest. So, instead of having large amounts of cash sitting in a current account earning no interest, you can set up daily electronic transfers to an interest-bearing account when the cash amount has reached a certain level. If your proposed business has an international dimension, you may well need to send and receive money from abroad. This needn't be complicated, and the small business adviser at your bank will be able to explain how it all works to keep your charges to a minimum.

Separating pots of money in this way is hugely beneficial to your understanding of how your business is faring. It is important to understand the distinction between cash flow and profit, and to set up the right metrics with which to determine your business health. The cash in your business may be no indication at all of likely profit. To give a simple example, you might proudly look at a bank statement saying that you have £20,000 in the bank. At an initial glance, this appears excellent, and very healthy. However, if you need to pay a supplier or the HM Revenue & Customs £19,000 next week, then the picture is less rosy. So the cash flowing through the business must not be confused with profit. Time lags are a significant danger here. Tax bills in particular come nine months after the event, and must be allowed for to avoid difficulty. This is where separate bank accounts for different purposes can be extremely helpful.

By taking advice from your bank and your accountant, you will be able to set up proper reporting systems that give you the full picture. It is important that you become familiar with what these figures are telling you. Cash flow shows what is in the account at the moment, but gives no indication of what needs to go out. All debts, bills, and other commitments need to be shown alongside the cash figure and offset against this cash income to give a better picture. Profit can be shown as a running percentage or expressed as margin on sales, but in truth is often only fully clear at the end of a year or sales period. Printouts of this information take a little getting used to, but there are some excellent software packages that can make this less daunting.

# WHO YOU NEED TO KNOW
## *Ingvar Kamprad*

Ingvar Kamprad, the founder of IKEA, began to develop a business as a young boy, selling matches to neighbours from his bicycle. He found that he could buy them in bulk very cheaply from Stockholm, sell them individually at a low price, and still make a good profit. From this modest base he expanded into selling fish, Christmas tree decorations, seeds, and ballpoint pens. When he was 17, his father gave him a cash reward for succeeding in his studies, and he used the money to establish what has grown into IKEA.

The acronym IKEA is made up of the initials of his name (IK) plus those of Elmtaryd, the family farm where he was born, and the nearby village of Agunnaryd. According to one Swedish business magazine he is the wealthiest person in the world, although this is based on the assumption that he owns the entire company, a fact that both he and IKEA dispute.

Nevertheless, his frugal approach to money is well known. He has lived in the same town in Switzerland since 1976, drives a 15-year-old Volvo, flies only economy class, encourages IKEA employees always to write on both sides of a piece of paper, and has even been known to visit IKEA for a 'cheap meal'. He is also believed to buy Christmas presents and wrapping paper in the post-Christmas sales. As such, he is arguably the living embodiment of the careful entrepreneur, for whom looking after the pennies has made the ultimate number of pounds.

# SECURING FINANCE

Start your business with an appropriate pot of money for what you are trying to achieve. You may need no upfront investment at all, and obviously you shouldn't borrow if you don't need to. But if you do, take the time to investigate the implications of having an overdraft, of borrowing, and of securing other finance.

Loans can be fixed or variable, and there are government-backed small loans guarantee schemes that could help. Securing finance can be challenging, and should be approached with care. All the business plan work that took place at the beginning needs to be well packaged and presented to whoever might be providing the funds. Often they will have their own format and detailed questionnaire, so your original format may need to be changed. The lender will need to be completely convinced of the validity of your idea and the likelihood of their being repaid, doubtless with interest.

Take the time to understand the motivations of the lender. Obviously you want the money, but why are they lending it to you and what is in it for them? The time period over which they expect repayment is crucial, and so are the repayment terms. Look hard at the time periods over which the loan must be repaid, and be realistic about the ability of your business to meet the deadline. Punitive interest rates are another pitfall, and have caused problems for many businesses. Even when you have secured an offer of a loan that both you and the lender are happy with, you might want to take legal advice before signing up, or to get a second opinion. Assuming all is fine, put safeguards in place for when the money comes through. Strong discipline is required to make sure that the funds are not spent too fast, or on things for which they were not intended.

Sometimes investment is needed for highly specific items that are critical to your business idea. You might need premises, particular machinery, vehicles, or other hardware that have to be financed if the business is to launch. The banks have experienced most of this before, and usually have particular types of finance schemes to suit. For example, if you need to buy or lease vehicles or premises, they will most likely have products that already fit the bill.

# TAX AND PAY

If you are a sole trader, but not a limited company, you will carry on paying tax twice a year in exactly the same way as you do with your personal tax. Bear in mind, though, that the amount the revenue requests in advance in January and July as 'on account' will change as earnings increase. So the more successful your business and the more money you take from it, the higher the tax bill. If you set up a limited company you will effectively have three tax bills to take care of – the two personal ones as usual, plus corporation tax once a year. The amount of this will be based on your annual income (which you will have to declare in your report and accounts), and is payable nine months after that year has closed. You can see straight away that this time lag is quite dangerous because the amount of cash in your bank account could make you believe all is well when in fact you have a looming corporation tax bill. It might therefore be wise to set up a separate fund specifically for the tax you know lies around the corner.

If you intend to employ staff, you need to become familiar with payment law, and that means a reasonable working knowledge of National Insurance, Pay-as-you earn (PAYE), employee benefits, your policy with regard to expense claims, pensions and much more. The HM Revenue & Customs website tells you everything you need to know about all of this (hmrc.gov.uk), and there are whole books dedicated to just this subject. At the beginning, it is good to have a clear idea of how you plan to pay salaries and dividends. If you are a sole trader, then you elect when you wish to take a dividend. This could be as regularly as once a month, or as infrequently as once a year. It's your choice, always assuming that you are not taking out more than the business can truly afford. If you have staff, then they will need to be paid a salary, and your business plan needs to allow for this every month. Depending on their pay level, the correct percentage of income tax needs to be deducted at source and paid to HMRC, along with their National Insurance contribution.

VAT (Value Added Tax) applies to all businesses with income of £60,000 or more. This may change, as does the rate of VAT, which has changed three times in the last three years. In January 2011 it moved to 20%. Once you have registered for VAT, you must add the relevant percentage to your invoices or product prices. You also need to keep a note of your costs and the amount of VAT you have paid out. Once a quarter you reconcile one against the other and pay the revenue. For small businesses, it is worth investigating the Flat Rate VAT Scheme.

This enables you to charge your customers at the standard rate, but pay the revenue less using a sliding scale based on the type of business you run. If you are in the scheme you pay this rate regardless and cannot reclaim any VAT. There is a ceiling on the size of business that qualifies for the scheme, currently gross income of £225,000 including VAT. Once again, all the details you need, along with the latest rates, are on the HMRC website.

# HOW TO HAVE A DECENT MARGIN

It is difficult to give general guidelines about how to handle money without distinguishing between service- and product-based businesses. If you produce or sell any form of product, then the basic equation of your business will be based on the cost of making or acquiring it in relation to the amount for which you sell it. That's your margin or, put another way, 'materials with mark-up'. Consider this principle in relation to your own business. Ask yourself:

- ▶ What level of mark-up will your customers accept?
- ▶ What can you do to make what you provide worth more?
- ▶ Do you have enough services on offer to increase your average margin?
- ▶ Is your pricing appropriate for what you provide?

The price–quality equation states that if they cost a lot, your products or services must be good. It takes confidence to determine your pricing this way, but if what you offer is genuinely high quality, then it makes good sense. What do you deduce about two products of similar type, one of which costs £2,000 and the other £200? The more expensive is probably better made and so of higher quality. It may have a cachet or brand value to which potential buyers aspire. There is nothing wrong with it being more expensive, assuming that there are people who appreciate those qualities and are prepared to pay for them. No matter how disparaging one chooses to be about products and services that are 'expensive', one is eventually forced to admit that, one way or another, there must be a market for them otherwise they would not remain in their market.

In which case, what would you deduce about two people, one of whom commands a fee of £2,000 a day, and the other £200? The more expensive is likely to be more experienced and therefore of higher quality. This is self-fulfilling, because if they are not, then in a fairly short space of time they will not generate any repeat business, and will fail as a business reasonably quickly. It may be something of a rhetorical question, but which of these two people would you rather be? Obviously it is a hypothetical example but the principle matters. If you cost a lot, then you must be good. This is the reaction that you should aspire to invoke in your customers and competitors. Clearly, there has to be an appropriate balance between price and delivery but, in the main, you should always place the maximum possible value on what you have to offer. If you are uncertain about what that value is, you need to test your pricing first. One of the helpful things about starting your own business is that you have the power to determine your own pricing. Examine any market and you will find this to be true. People like paying for high quality goods and services. So look carefully at the equation between price and quality, and consider premium prices that are justified. Don't sell yourself cheap.

Another facet of retaining a healthy margin is to be canny about requests for free or 'win only' work. 'Share in our success or failure' was one of the more unfortunate traits of the dot com boom in the late 1990s. This is a euphemism for a customer saying 'I won't pay for anything unless things have gone really well and I decide that I can afford it'. The main rule here is never to give anything away for free, unless you have an overwhelming reason to do so. When people ask why you won't do speculative work for free, the best answer is 'Because I don't need to'. They really have no response to that.

Although there is usually no reason to give your time away for free, you may reserve the right to charge less or provide free work if you deem that it is appropriate. You will be the best judge of any given state of affairs, and the joy of running your own business is that it is your decision to make. Here are some possible reasons why you might want to provide something free or at a reduced price:

▶ Because it will lead to repeat business
▶ Because it will lead to new business
▶ Because it is part of a much bigger deal
▶ Because they are a highly-valued customer
▶ Because you can.

A final thought on free work. If you have had a really good sales period, why not offer to work free for a charity or a worthy cause for a limited period, or give them a one-off delivery of your product? Your expertise may be of significantly greater value than any donation you might ordinarily make, and may even be more useful than cash.

## WHO YOU NEED TO KNOW
### *Chris Anderson*

Chris Anderson is Editor-in-Chief of *Wired* magazine and author of two important books, *The Long Tail* and *Free*. Both have won numerous business book awards, and each has a particular point to make in relation to the way businesses make money in the modern world.

First, he asserted that the future of business does not lie in 'hits' – the high-volume end of a traditional demand curve – but in what used to be regarded as the misses – the seemingly endless long tail of that same curve. As the world is transformed by the internet and the near-infinite choice it offers, it is his view that the aggregated niches in the tail represent a better business opportunity than an attempt to have a hit.

Second, he suggested that, if something is digital, then sooner or later it's going be free. Online businesses need to appreciate this, but there is no need to panic because it is possible to embrace the idea of giving some things away whilst still making good money. Sooner or later most businesses have to compete with free, so this is an important part of thinking when looking at viability and margin.

It is worth noting that his theories do not meet with universal approval. Some point out that the long tail principle applies predominantly to online businesses, and less so, or not at all, to traditional ones. The free theory is equally controversial and many businesses have quite reasonably attempted to demonstrate the opposite – that generating significant demand and charging a premium price avoids the need for offering anything for free.

# COPING IN A DOWNTURN

Recent world events have caused many to ask whether it is a good idea to start a business during a downturn. The figures actually show that more start-ups succeed when they start in tough times than those that don't. This may be something to do with starting prudently and keeping things that way in your business, rather than starting with a more relaxed, or even cavalier attitude. Assuming times are at the tougher end of the spectrum, there are certain approaches that start-ups can take to stand a better than average chance of success. Most of it is to do with attitude. It may be tough medicine, but it works. Here are six suggestions.

## 1. Don't 'do gloomy'

No one wants to listen to someone moaning. The circumstances might be difficult, but you don't have to be miserable. If you are, you will probably lose customers fast.

## 2. Don't invoke a higher power

Bad performers often use the context of a recession to claim that their company's poor performance is nothing to do with them – it's the economy, apparently. This isn't always true.

## 3. You only need one girlfriend

Complaining that there is no work is like a man saying there are no women in his town. You only need one girlfriend or piece of work, so go and find it.

## 4. Good companies do the right things all the time

There is no difference between the things your business should do in a recession versus what you should be doing in any other circumstances. If you have to ask what to do differently in a recession, then it may actually be too late.

## 5. Sometimes things go up, and sometimes they go down

Economies go up and down. You still need to earn a living, so you need to believe that your success is entirely in your own hands, and go for it.

## 6. Nip into the gap

You need to be dexterous enough to nip into the gaps that other businesses might have missed by being too cautious. Be flexible and keep coming up with new ideas.

## WHO SAID IT

"If you can count your money, you don't have a billion dollars."
– John Paul Getty

## LOOKING AHEAD TO AVOID A CRISIS

Looking back can help you to look forward, and often the experience gained can help avoid a crisis at some point in the future. Being retrospective doesn't mean losing perspective. Considering the past doesn't necessarily mean indulging in nostalgia. In fact, many people who run their own businesses repeat their mistakes precisely because they don't review the past and learn anything from it.

Even in the earliest days of your business – perhaps in a test market – it pays to look back at all the customers you have had and what products or services you have provided for them. The frequency with which you do this rather depends on the nature of your business. In a

fast-moving business that involves many customer transactions a day, this might be as often as weekly. Fashion
retailers look at their sales figures every Monday, and
adjust pricing and product mix immediately to rectify
problems or capitalize on opportunities. You may be able
to do the same.

Reviewing the past objectively can give you some fantastic
ideas and insights, based on what you have already done.
Large organizations have data and records to draw on,
but when you run your own business you may only have
a very limited amount of information. In fact, a lot of it
might even be in your head. Start by jotting down the
overall shape of your business:

- ► What was your total income last week or month?
- ► What were your costs?
- ► What was your profit?
- ► How many customers did you have?
- ► How many jobs or transactions did you
  complete?
- ► What was the highest value transaction?
- ► What was the lowest?
- ► What was the average?
- ► What was the average value of a customer?
- ► Is the trend going up or down?
- ► Is the customer mix right?
- ► Are the number of transactions per customer
  appropriate?
- ► Is the level of repeat purchase acceptable?
- ► Is the cost per job viable?

▶ Is the value per customer adequate?

▶ What are the important things that need to change?

Anyone who runs their own business needs to have a firm and up-to-date grip on these matters. As a rough rule of thumb, if you aren't broadly aware of the answers to these types of questions, then you may not be sufficiently on top of your business. Equally, if something you offer proves to be very popular, it is vital that you work out why. Differentiate between the types of products that you have sold, and group them along the lines of what you sold most, what you sold the least, what the different types of product are, their viability, their enjoyment and satisfaction for you and your staff, and so on. Looking at these questions could help you to re-engineer your business on your own terms. If the things you enjoy most make the most money, then you are in luck (or you are a master of balancing work and pleasure). If not, consider whether you can change the proportion of less enjoyable and lower margin jobs for ones that make better economic and satisfaction sense. You really do owe this to yourself, and should be able to arrange the money–enjoyment balance more to your liking.

Naturally, if something you offer doesn't generate enough profit, then you need to work out why as fast as possible. So the flip side of this exercise is to identify things that you sell or do that actually don't make enough money. Many businesses produce huge quantities of work or products in a particular area only to conclude that they are neither viable nor that enjoyable to provide. This is why regular reviews are important, otherwise you could be spending your time on something that you don't necessarily like doing, and which doesn't even bring in worthwhile money. Asking tough questions now will help avoid problems in the future. Be honest with yourself, and if something you offer doesn't make enough money, work out why and make the necessary decisions.

- ▶ What would happen if you stopped doing that thing?
- ▶ Would the business suffer in any way?
- ▶ Would more time be released for you to do more enjoyable or profitable things?
- ▶ Would anyone notice or care?
- ▶ Would the quality of your working life improve?
- ▶ Would the quality of your personal life improve?

This level of questioning summarizes the type of quizzical approach you should always adopt in relation to the financial aspects of your business. It represents the heart of whether it will be a success or not. But do not turn money matters into a permanent obsession. It is far better to concentrate on running the business well, and the likelihood is that the money will flow as a result. Keep an eye on which products represent the greatest margin opportunity, and examine regularly whether this needs adjustment. A deep understanding of what has proved popular and viable before will inform your decisions about what to do next.

# WHAT YOU NEED TO READ

► The main online resource for everything relating to tax, VAT and pay is *www.hmrc.gov.uk*, the site of HM Revenue and Customs.

► *Small Business Finance All-in-One For Dummies* by Faith Glasgow (John Wiley and Sons Ltd) is a good place to start for all things financial.

► Peter Taylor's *Book-keeping and Accounting for the Small Business: How to Keep the Books and Maintain Financial Control Over Your Business* (How To Books) contains much more detail, and specific advice on the intricacies of bookkeeping.

► *What You See Is What You Get* (Pan MacMillan) is Alan Sugar's autobiography, and provides a no-nonsense account of how to concentrate on the right products at the right price.

► *The Real Deal: My Story from Brick Lane to Dragons' Den* (Virgin Books) is James Caan's life story, and should provide inspiration for anyone starting a business from scratch. We all have to start somewhere, and his approach is salutary. After dropping out of school at just sixteen, he started his business life in a broom cupboard with no qualifications and two pieces of fatherly wisdom: 'observe the masses and do the opposite', and 'always look for opportunities where both parties benefit'. Sound advice indeed.

▶ Chris Anderson's two books *Free* and *The Long Tail* (Random House) explain in detail how niche businesses can make good money without having to fear the large corporations. *Free* examines in particular how the presence of so much free competitive product can be used to your advantage.

# IF YOU ONLY REMEMBER ONE THING

Don't shy away from the money bit. Keep a close eye on margin rather than just sales, and determine your optimum pricing to make your business as profitable as possible.

# CHAPTER 5

# SALES AND MARKETING

## WHAT IT'S ALL ABOUT

- ▶ Designing a contact strategy
- ▶ Reviewing your marketing
- ▶ Describing what you do
- ▶ Successful online marketing
- ▶ Effective sales meetings and networking

There are lots of businesses that do not bother with marketing. They leave communication to chance. Is this a good thing? Who cares if your business communicates well? Does it have any bearing on your fortunes? Can you live without marketing? Most companies wrestle with these issues at some point in their development. What happens if you choose *not* to communicate adequately? Nothing disastrous, you might reasonably conclude. However, as your business grows, so will its reputation, and a reputation is a fragile bundle of opinions that could have a significant bearing on your success. The problem is that if you decide to say nothing, customers will simply draw their own conclusions. Their view of your business may be accurate and well informed, but then again it might not. So it is better to design it in a style that suits your needs rather than leave it to chance.

# MARKETING MATTERS

All of your effort so far could prove irrelevant if you don't bother to tell anybody about your business and what it has to offer. Your business is going to develop a reputation whether you like it or not, and this is likely to be determined by:

- ▶ How *you* behave personally
- ▶ How you *tell* people you behave
- ▶ How you tell *your* people to behave (if you have them)
- ▶ How your products deliver

It all starts with you. You need to tell anyone who will listen what type of business you are. That's half the battle. Then tell your staff (if you have them). They need to behave in a way that is appropriate to what you stand for, and what you believe to be right. They can only do this if they are told what is expected of them. And, of course, you need to behave that way yourself.

How much should you spend on sales and marketing? First, we need to examine the distinction between sales and marketing. In the purest sense, sales are purely financial transactions, and in theory they can occur in the absence of marketing. Equally, marketing can generate a lot of activity publicizing products and services, but not actually lead to any sales. In this respect, they can be viewed as separate items, but in most companies they are not. The two disciplines are generally regarded as indivisible – marketing should always lead to sales, and sales usually needs the help of marketing. Most organizations therefore now combine the two things. Much has been written about appropriate marketing investment levels. As a rough rule of thumb, mature companies that embrace marketing as a discipline spend 8–13% of their turnover on it. They don't do this for fun, but for hard-nosed commercial reasons that have been proven to improve their fortunes. Most modern companies have concluded that there is essentially no difference between marketing and sales. As such, they believe that to have 'no marketing' is to abdicate from sales altogether. The answer for small businesses may be quite different. There is a huge difference between paid-for marketing and free marketing. Your most powerful weapon in the early days is you. You need to get out and about and promote what you do vigorously. To start with, you may not have to spend any money on marketing at all.

Start by saying hello to everyone who could help. It is extraordinary the number of people who haven't even bothered to let everyone know what they do for a living. This is one of the most powerful forms of marketing, and yet many leave it out completely. Word of mouth is free, and much more persuasive than any marketing you might pay for. Everybody you meet could be a potential customer, but that isn't the main point. Far more important is the fact that, even if they don't want what you have to offer, they might know someone who does. Creating a buzz around what you do is important, and it needn't cost anything.

The same goes for when you need help in the early days. Don't be afraid to ask for small favours from people to get you going. This applies to marketing as much as to painting the walls of your first office or shop. Do you have any contacts who could help spread the word about what you do? Would they mind if you promoted your business on their premises? Think broadly about the possibilities – the chances are, they will say yes. And don't forget to return the favour when they need one from you.

## WHO SAID IT

"Without promotion something terrible happens: nothing."
– P. T. Barnum

# CRUCIAL SALES AND MARKETING INSIGHTS

You should plan a sales and marketing strategy first. This is the big picture, and should not be confused with the tactics, the activity itself or particular initiatives. Your overall approach needs to be considered before you get into detail, and when starting a business there are a number of crucial insights that can be gleaned from the huge amount written on the subject. Important lessons include:

1. *Marketing is not complicated.*
   It is surrounded by an industry and much mystique, but for small businesses it can actually be quite straightforward.

2. *Marketing plans can be simple.*
   Vast marketing plans are unlikely to be of much help to the small business. Stick to simple ideas that are easy to understand and implement.

3. *Marketing doesn't have to take long.*
   You can write your approach on the back of a napkin and be enacting it next week.

4. *Marketing doesn't have to cost much.*
   It can even be free. Consider all the free options before you spend any valuable cash, especially in the early days.

5. *Marketing isn't a panacea.*
   It may not solve all your business issues, but if you don't let people know what you are offering you are probably missing a significant opportunity.

6. *Marketing strategy needn't be daunting.*
   It is just a word for describing what you have decided to do.

7. *People actually like paying for products and services.*
   As long as they are high quality and you give them a reason to justify it.

8. *All your staff have a role to play in marketing.*
   Every time they talk to anyone outside the company, they are marketing.

9. *In tough times, ignore the 80:20 rule.*
   Some marketers advocate applying 80% of your effort to 20% of your customer base. Instead, market hard to your top 1%. You will

save time, and are more likely to keep your margin.

10. *In tough times, be brave.*
    The braver you are, the greater the likely sales result.

# THE VALUE OF PRE-MARKETING

Pre-marketing is another helpful idea for priming the sales pump. One of the most frequent problems with marketing is that people leave it far too late. Of course, it depends on the nature of what your business is selling, but often people need time to think about what they might need from you. Particularly if your products are premium-priced, they won't necessarily make a snap decision based on 30 seconds of chat from you or a colleague. If you can acknowledge this early on, then you can build that consideration time into your plan. Impulse purchases are fine, but higher value and low frequency items need thought. Pre-marketing means letting people know what you can do for them, or provide them with, long before you actually want their custom. In the early days you may find this difficult because you want the sale quickly, but it doesn't take long for you to build a pipeline of interest that could materialize at some later point in the future. Start this process now, and your efforts will be less desperate later. Once you have prepared your strategy, you can get into the detail of what the specific tactics are that you plan to enact. Here are some ideas:

1. *Start with the basics.*

   Think about what you actually want to achieve and define your objectives clearly. Make sure you seek out the right people in the right way to get the best results. It is important to listen to your customers and their needs to ensure that your product or service really satisfies their requirements.

2. *Get connected.*

   Consider placing your business in a directory, such as the Yellow Pages, local business directories such as the Chamber of Commerce, or local web directories. It may seem obvious, but with a one-off payment each year you can reach anyone who is directly looking for your product or service.

3. *DIY public relations.*

   PR is the art of getting 'free' publicity, even if it proves necessary to pay an agency to achieve it for you. The aim is to persuade a publication or media channel to feature your product or service favourably in their editorial. Sometimes they are actively looking for ideas, so you can make a start by writing your own press releases in the manner of a news story and sending it to your local papers and business magazines.

4. *Be creative.*

   Creative services do not have to cost a fortune. Agencies that specialize in working with small businesses are often flexible and good value. Try sharing costs and creative ideas with other local firms who are in a similar situation.

5. *Improve your website.*

Constructing a website can cost as little as a few hundred pounds but it is a vital marketing tool. Customers now expect to see a website as much as they do a brochure. Failing that, you may be able to replicate the same features on a free blog. Huge numbers of people now investigate businesses on the web first, so a website is effectively mandatory. This is the place where you can explain all your products and services, and customers can choose the level of detail they are after, and how long they wish to spend investigating them. Also bear in mind that a bad or out-of-date website is as bad as none at all.

6. *Keep in touch.*

Newsletters and emails are a very effective way of reminding your customers of your presence, as well as giving you the chance to promote new products or pass on news about your business. However, only contact those by email who have specifically given you permission.

7. *Encourage word of mouth.*

Offer your existing customers incentives to recommend you to others. Send out a referral form with each delivery or invoice, making it as easy as possible for your customers to do so. Also include testimonials from existing customers on your website and business literature.

8. *Try something new.*

   The internet is a good resource for marketing, but you have to make your business stand out. Try using a pay-per-click service on a search engine. Each click can cost as little as a few pence.

9. *Show off.*

   Trade exhibitions provide an ideal place to meet your customers and potential clients face to face, and they usually give you a chance to check out the competition. Looking at what works and what doesn't for others can help you avoid making expensive mistakes yourself.

10. *Learn from the past.*

    Analyze which marketing efforts were effective and which were not, and ask yourself why, in order to refine and improve next year's marketing.

To summarize, marketing is simply the regular explanation of what you do to anyone who will listen. It can be free, and if you can keep it that way, then so much the better. Keep going again and again with new ideas. There is no point in your business being beautifully run on the one hand and the world's best kept secret on the other. Spread the word. Let the world know.

# WHO YOU NEED TO KNOW
## *Adam Morgan*

Adam Morgan is the author of *Eating the Big Fish* and *The Pirate Inside*. He began life working in advertising agencies in the 1980s and 1990s, and for the last decade or so has run his own company called Eat Big Fish. He has pioneered and invented astute methods for challenger brands – those that are smaller and have fewer resources than the so-called big fish. Big fish are brand leaders, and challengers are everyone else. Clearly, there are more of the latter than the former, but most marketing theory up until then was written about the leaders and so was barely applicable for the challengers. Based on the Avis principle of 'When you're only number two you try harder', his ideas are an inspiration for any small business feeling somewhat daunted by bigger and better-established competition.

Of particular relevance to starting a business is the idea of sacrifice and overcommit. Sacrifice means not doing lots of things you would like to, and overcommit means putting extra effort into the one thing you have chosen to do.

So these two sides of the same coin refer to sacrificing marketing initiatives that seem attractive but which will actually dissipate the central effort, and then adding every conceivable resource to 'overcommiting' to the one effort. In other words, choose one thing, ditch the rest, and throw your full weight behind it for maximum effect.

The books contain lots of techniques and explain how you can run your own session to decide on your most appropriate strategy.

# DESIGNING A CONTACT STRATEGY

So having turned your mind to marketing matters, investigated a number of important insights for your business, and considered the pre-marketing element, you need to move on to designing a contact strategy. Your contact strategy is your lifeblood. It all starts with your initial contact list. Here you need to write down everyone you know with whom you could possibly do business, and with whom you could get in touch. Ideally, it should only include the name of the person, the company and the date you last made contact with them. Don't be tempted to add other information – it will only distract you from the simple matter of contacting them. If you really do feel that you need more information, then note it somewhere else. Do not be tempted to enhance the list with extraneous detail. It has no bearing on the likelihood of you making the call, organizing a meeting, or achieving the thing that needs to be done – it only blurs your ability to get on with the task in hand. Every time you speak to someone or meet up with them, write the date down and move their details to the top of the list. This becomes your ready-made recall system.

After a suitable period of time has elapsed, draw a Pester Line at a certain date when you believe it is appropriate to call again. If you do it more than once a month, you are probably pestering, but the appropriate frequency will depend on the nature of your business. Every six months is likely to be ideal in a service business where you are involved in one or two projects a year. But if you leave it a year, many of your contacts will have left the company or changed their job description. Work out a frequency of contact that suits the nature of your business, and adjust it if it doesn't seem to be working.

The number of people on your contact list needs constant scrutiny. If there are more than 500 at the outset, you are most likely fooling yourself or spreading yourself too thinly. It is much better to have a smaller number of viable, genuine prospects than a huge list full of people you don't really know. Keep a constant eye on your frequency of contact. If you overdo it, after a period of receiving your (perhaps unwanted) solicitations, you will begin to tarnish your reputation (in other words, you will have overstepped the Pester Line). Or you will simply dissipate too much of your time on people who aren't interested in what you have to offer.

On the other hand, if there are less than 100 contacts on the list at the outset, your business may not be viable. You need a decent universe against which to apply the normal laws of probability. If you are absolutely charmed, it is possible that you could sustain a living on five customers who give you precisely the amount of work that you want exactly when you need it. That's very unlikely, although it might just be feasible in a service industry where you have an established reputation that provides a ready-made flow of work. Much more likely is a selection of potential customers who don't actually give you work despite regular promises; work which does eventually arrive but much later than you expected; projects that turn out to be much smaller than anticipated when they do eventually arrive, and so on. If you sell a product, you may to a certain degree be at the whim of various market forces, a series of random factors, and the possible effectiveness of whatever offers and promotions you decide to run. Therefore, it is better if you can generate your own pipeline to even out all these variations.

# REVIEWING YOUR MARKETING

Your new business hit list is an essential system. This is the list that you generate once your contact list has taken shape. You need to think carefully and very broadly about anyone who could have a bearing on the success of your business. This is not a cynical exercise in exploitation. It is merely casting the net as wide as possible to make the most of the potential contacts that you have. Reviewing this list needs to become part of your system. Constantly review it to see if you could be generating new opportunities. Refine your thinking regularly by asking direct questions:

▶ Where are you likely to have most success?
▶ Why is a certain approach not working?
▶ What new approach might work?
▶ How can you apply one set of skills to another market?
▶ Have you overlooked an obvious source of business?
▶ What type of work do you enjoy most?
▶ Where do you make the best margin?
▶ Which examples of previous work are most impressive?

Now start getting the list into some sort of priority order. Put the hottest prospects at the top and revise the order when things change. Keep the numbers manageable. Any less than ten prospects on your hit list and you may not achieve the progress you want. More than 50 and you might faze yourself and do nothing, rather like facing a plate with too much food on it. If you have trouble tackling a list of this size, break it down into manageable chunks that suit you – groups of six or ten perhaps. Try colour-coding them so that you can distinguish one set from the other. If your first system doesn't work, simply admit it and invent a new one. Remember, the system is entirely for your own convenience. Just make it work for you.

Keep inventing new ideas for contacting prospective customers. You need to be vigilant about issues and trends. Pick up on articles in the trade press. Track movements of people and ideas. It works well when you ring up and say that you have noticed something relevant to them and have a suggestion. It shows that you are on the ball, and makes it easier to get work. If you are selling products, keep re-analyzing their appeal to your customer base.

- ▶ What is 'in' at the moment?
- ▶ Do your products fit that mood?
- ▶ Can you extend your range?
- ▶ What if you run a promotion?
- ▶ What if you alter your pricing?
- ▶ How about some local marketing?
- ▶ Are your marketing materials out of date or looking a little tired?
- ▶ Are there any seasonal events that you should be capitalizing on?

Just because someone didn't buy your first suggestion doesn't mean they won't buy your second. Things change all the time. Bright ideas appropriately suggested are always interesting to people. Keep coming up with new ones. Every time you contact someone, move them to your contact list. The definition of a contact is a meeting or a proper phone conversation. At bare minimum you will have explained who you are, provided your details and discussed the possibility of work at some point in the future. Never have someone on your contact list who should be on your new business hit list. They are not a genuine contact until you have spoken to them properly or met them and discussed at least the vague possibility of them becoming a customer.

You should aim for 50 percent repeat business within three years. You should expect your customers to be pleased with what you offer so you should expect further custom in due course. If you are selling products, there is still a service element to what you do, and your objective must be to have your customers coming back. Even accounting for the random availability of projects, seasonal factors and the cyclical nature of certain markets, you should always aspire to get more business from at least half of your existing customers. You should also track satisfied customers when they move house, move to new jobs or have a change of circumstances. Whatever has happened, they will be confronted by a whole new set of issues, many of which you may be able to address. In a service business in particular, it is important to go and have a coffee with people when they move. It is flattering for them, it gives you a flavour of their new set-up, and there is always something new to discuss.

# WHO YOU NEED TO KNOW

*Richard Reed, Adam Balon and Jon Wright*

Innocent Drinks is a business phenomenon of the last decade. Founded in 1998 by three college friends, it grew at an amazing rate to become the UK's fastest growing food and drink business in 2005. Equally impressive has been the growth of its brand legend. Innocent is one of those brands that everyone in the marketing world refers to with awe, affection and sometimes envy.

The story of Innocent's rise centres on Reed, Balon and Wright, and their unique approach to marketing. The company's open and chatty style has made it a brand that people observe, love and (increasingly) try to imitate – everything from pack copy jokingly suggesting that the ingredients included a helicopter to the Innocent cow vans touring the country. Reed and his colleagues have truly established a brand that is known for its love of storytelling, sense of humour and an honest approach to business.

There are many sales and marketing lessons to be learnt from Innocent. Being open and honest with customers is one, as demonstrated when they set up their first stall at a music festival and asked purchasers to vote on whether their smoothies were any good or not. Another is retaining a sense of normality with which people can empathize. Of course your product needs to be good, but great marketing can certainly help your chances of success.

# DESCRIBING WHAT YOU DO

You won't have a business unless you let people know who you are, where you are, and what you do. You need to know where to find your customers, and how to communicate with them. You need to become adept at describing what you do, preferably in less than 30 seconds. Potential customers may not be interested in listening for more than a minute. This is true at an interview, a drinks party, in the pub, at the squash club – anywhere, in fact. After that, they become bored. You need to come across in a lucid, enthusiastic way. Start by writing down what you do in no more than three sentences. Now read it out loud. Does it sound daft? If so, rewrite it. Try again. Does it sound like a cliché? Does it sound like all the other claims you read in corporate brochures? If so, change it. Make it fun and engaging. Do it with some pride and a lot of energy. Now you can use it for face-to-face conversations, telephone calls and all your written work. Also bear in mind that this should evolve constantly to keep pace with the manner in which your business develops. Broadly speaking, no one cares what you do to earn a living. It's your job to express it clearly so everyone can understand and, ideally, to make it interesting and appealing. If you can't, why should anyone else bother to try to understand it?

When drawing together your marketing materials, do introduce some character into the manner in which you describe your company and your products. Interesting things start to happen when you do. Most modern markets have a tremendous amount of competition, so it is extremely likely that there is another business somewhere that offers pretty much the same as yours. If this is true, then prospective customers may be confronted with competitors offering similar goods, location, price, delivery times, and so on, to yours. With all these factors being roughly equal, they may well make their decision based on the brand character that you and your company choose to emanate. This is where your marketing comes into its own.

The proposition you developed in Chapter 2 forms the basis of how to describe your business. Combined with your personal character, it will become the cornerstone of your marketing materials. There should be good consistency between all the elements – website, logo, brochures, leaflets, packaging, mailings, and so on. Ideally, a customer should be able to look at any of these and recognize a clear similarity of style, or family feel. This usually happens when you view all the elements as different manifestations of one central thought, rather than a haphazard collection of items all conceived at different times. Bear in mind that in the early days things will probably change quite rapidly and so should the manner in which you describe what you do. The chances are that your marketing materials will become obsolete pretty quickly. So update them. It doesn't have to be an expensive exercise if you stick to the basics and concentrate on the elements that work well in your market. At an appropriate moment, do pause to consider:

- ▶ What do you think of the materials?
- ▶ Do they accurately represent what you do these days?
- ▶ Which initiatives worked and which didn't?
- ▶ What can you learn from that?
- ▶ Do you use some elements more than others?
- ▶ Has the emphasis of your business changed?

▶ Is there any point in producing something new?

So, shortly after launch you should consider rewriting your marketing materials. What you said about your business two months ago might not be how you would phrase it now. Equally, just because a marketing initiative didn't work before doesn't mean it won't work now. If your business develops fast, your existing material is probably out of date, so re-examine it. Many businesses send out one launch mailing and then sit back thinking that they have 'done marketing'. The market is changing all the time. People come and go. Products and tastes change. You can never conclusively prove that something that didn't work before won't work now. Choose your medium carefully. You may decide to use different media for different messages. Whatever you do, don't just fire off an email to all your contacts and assume that the business will roll in. As well as materials, don't forget the power of talking. It is your job to stay very close to them and the markets in which you operate. When you have some new ideas that you want to test, talk to your customers. Ask them:

▶ What else could I do for you?
▶ Did you realize that what I do for you is only a fraction of what I do for some of my other customers?
▶ What are the main things preoccupying you at the moment that I could help with?

► Would you like me to investigate something new for you?
► Are you dissatisfied with any suppliers who provide similar services to me?
► Do you know any other potential customers who might want to use my services or products?
► What could I do better?

Ask open-ended questions and pay attention to their responses. The new selling opportunities are usually lurking in the answers given. Let your customers talk. In many instances, they will invent new ideas and opportunities for you on the spot. Occasionally drop in new ideas. Offer to develop a thought into a proposal. Suggest that you do a little development work on a subject and follow up to see if it is worth proceeding. In the modern business world they call this being proactive. In truth it is simply having ideas and getting things done.

## WHO SAID IT

"Every sale has five basic obstacles: no need, no money, no hurry, no desire, no trust."
– Zig Ziglar

# SUCCESSFUL ONLINE MARKETING

Harnessing the powerful potential of social media is another important marketing tool at your disposal. First, it is important to understand the 'new rules'. The knack to social media marketing is to forget the old rules of traditional marketing and think the opposite. Social media is about engaging in grown-up dialogue with your customers and potential clients, not simply churning out promotional messages. That means having a conversation, listening hard, being open and transparent, being authentic, and being generous with your expertise and knowledge. It does not mean broadcasting, shouting the loudest, being secretive about your company's workings, bragging or being mean and competitive.

Now consider your online strategy. Although social media marketing shouldn't feel overly promotional, it does serve a very important commercial purpose. Like all marketing, therefore, it should be embarked upon in a strategic way and with a clear plan in mind. Before diving in it is important to ask yourself some basic questions:

- ▶ With whom do I want to communicate?
- ▶ How do I want to come across?
- ▶ What do I want to achieve from my activity?
- ▶ What resources do I have?

Before embarking on social media marketing, you should take some time to review the functionality of your website.

This is a primary sales tool. Consider online appointment making programmes, merchandise sales, newsletter, and blog feed subscription tools – all of which will help with data capture. You might also want to create a blog. Your blog is a place to show off your personality and expertise in a dynamic, modern way. Wordpress, Blogger and Typepad are all very user-friendly and make it easy to set up a blog, which you can link from your website. Bear in mind that people are likely to remember just 10% of what they read but 50% of what they see and hear, so you can use video podcasts to demonstrate your products. Don't worry if these are not professionally shot, because home-style video content gives the impression of honesty and authenticity.

Consider setting up a company page on Facebook and using new features such as the 'Like' function to increase your brand awareness. Include photos, videos, customer feedback and your blog feed if you have them. You can also set up on LinkedIn. Up until recently only personal profiles could be set up on this site, but now it allows company profiles with a new 'Follow us' function. Also investigate the 'Groups' function to expand your business network and identify potential new product partners, business alliances and affiliations. Twitter is another possibility. The fact that updates on Twitter are restricted to 140 characters does not mean that they should purely be about what you had for your lunch today. Take time to understand Twitter: how to use @links, Retweets (RTs), trending topics and #hashtags. If you do use this medium, make sure you vary your tweets – share your own articles from your blog, share breaking news, Retweet others, give the odd personal update, ask for volunteer mystery shoppers, and offer some promotions. With all of this, you will soon find your number of followers increasing.

With all online initiatives, it is important to be realistic. The beauty of social media marketing is that most of it is free. It does, however, require a big time commitment to get it right. Before you start, consider how much time you can commit and keep within your capabilities. Better to have a small, select online presence done well, than abandoned Twitter sites, barren Facebook pages, and blog posts last updated years ago. If you can set aside an hour a day though, they might just prove to be the most productive hours of the week.

# EFFECTIVE SALES MEETINGS AND NETWORKING

Remember that in general people give business to those whom they like meeting. The purpose of a meeting is to establish a relationship, to propose something, or to agree something. Don't set up meetings for the sake of it. Always ask yourself: 'What's the point?' Be sharp and lively, and establish a reputation as a person with whom a meeting is always a pleasure. You want your customers to be saying: 'Whenever I have a meeting with you I get something out of it.'

When you start out, you do actually need to meet quite a lot of people. This is because the law of averages dictates that you need a reasonable critical mass of contacts to make any business work. In the early days, the shape of your business will not be sharply defined (no matter how rigorous you were in the planning stages), so you need to stay open-minded. Moreover, bear in mind that every meeting you have involves a judgement of character as well as an assessment of someone's technical skills. The more people you communicate with, the more experience you will have of working out whether you will get on well with them, and whether they will be relevant to your aspirations for your business.

Once you have met a number of people, you can refine your approach into some proper networking. This is not a cynical process whereby you extract all the benefits from people and give them nothing back. In some quarters, the very word 'networking' has as bad a reputation as 'sales'. But properly executed networking should benefit everyone. There is a difference between meeting a lot of people and networking. In the early days, you need to meet lots of people and stay open-minded. When you have built up some experience of their capabilities and aspirations, you can network. This will involve keeping in contact with those who could benefit from your skills and vice versa, at a frequency that is appropriate to your line of work and how busy they are. You keep in touch, help them out, suggest things and, ideally, do business together. Everyone wins.

If you are in a service business with a small number of significant customers, take them to lunch and insist on paying. It could be lunch. It could be breakfast, dinner, the races or even just a drink. The thing is that social surroundings promote a totally different mood than those of a meeting room, many of which appear to be designed precisely to reduce the chances of meetings being enjoyable. Suggesting a social get-together is a constructive, magnanimous thing to do. It says that you are broad-minded, that you are interested in other aspects of your customers than just their money, and that you can afford it.

In this way, you will be engineering a situation in which you can show your generosity, your interest in the client and, quite possibly, the degree to which you are on the ball with your suggestions of places to go and things to do. What do you talk about when you meet up? A bit of business, certainly. But mainly simply ask short, open-ended questions and then listen. You'll be amazed what comes up. People will talk when they are put at ease. They will talk about their families and relationships, their concerns, their feelings about their job, sport, hobbies, current affairs – pretty much anything. Of course, there are some bores in the world, but in the main there are interesting things to learn and discuss. The more ideas you have, the smarter you will appear, not because you are faking it but because it will be true. It's all part of honing good communication skills.

So marketing does matter, but it doesn't have to be daunting or complicated, particularly for small businesses. Stick to home truths about what your business can offer, and try a series of short, fast initiatives. Learn from their effect, and gradually build up your experience of what works in your market.

## WHAT YOU NEED TO READ

▶ *www.eatbigfish.com* is a free community resource featuring a range of techniques, interviews and stories to inspire and inform.

▶ *Innocent: Building a Brand from Nothing But Fruit* by John Simmons (Marshall Cavendish) is the inspiring story of how Innocent Drinks became the fastest growing food and drink business in the UK.

▶ Patrick Forsyth's *Marketing Stripped Bare* (Kogan Page) is a concise and witty primer on all things marketing related.

▶ *Marketing Judo* by John Barnes and Richard Richardson (Prentice Hall) explains how you can build your business using brains rather than just budget.

# IF YOU ONLY REMEMBER ONE THING

It is essential to let people know who you are, where you are, and what you do.

# CHAPTER 6

# PEOPLE

## WHAT IT'S ALL ABOUT ➡

- ▶ Creating a team shape
- ▶ Recruiting the right people
- ▶ Keeping them motivated
- ▶ How to deal with problems
- ▶ Sustaining relationships

Without people, the world would certainly be a dull place. Business cannot function without them. So the truism that every business is a people business needs careful examination. Those starting their own business who plan to work on their own face a particular set of circumstances. They will need to motivate themselves and be capable of working in isolation, which does not appeal to everybody. We will deal with some of these issues, and the lifestyle choices that they represent, in Chapter 8. So this chapter is dedicated to those who intend to start a business involving partners, colleagues or staff. Hiring and looking after these people takes a lot of time and attention.

Before we get into the detail, we need to revisit an important element of the original plan. In the same way that you will have decided whether you need to borrow money at all to start out, you will also have had to ask whether you need any people at all. Your business may require other people, but it might not. Careful thought at the beginning can make a huge difference to costs, morale and effectiveness. 'High maintenance' members of staff are one of the most time-consuming issues in any business. No one is suggesting that you become a hermit, and perhaps your business genuinely cannot function without a workforce. However, if you are working for yourself, you do at least have the option to consider structuring a business that minimizes the effect others can have on your fortunes. You owe it to yourself to consider whether there is any possibility that you could run your business without anyone else. If there is any chance that you might, it is a strongly recommended option that will enable you to make clearer and faster decisions, avoid having to deal with politics, or having to handle relationships with colleagues.

# CREATING A TEAM SHAPE

Let's assume you have decided that you *do* need to work with others to make your plan a success. Your first issue to address is the shape of the team. Consider the definition of a team: it's a group of players forming one of the sides in a sporting contest, or, in this case, a group of people organized to work together. You will want to know what the skills needs are, who complements whom, who can cover for whom, and what the optimum combination is. Take a blank sheet of paper and design what would work best. Consider your favourite team in any walk of life and work out what makes them so admirable. Then try to create something that emulates its qualities. You'll want to make sure that there is a sensible balance of empowerment and ownership in it. Analyze your own skills and hand some of your responsibilities over, particularly those tasks you are less good at. Many of the tasks that you regard as menial will be regarded by others as interesting new challenges, so don't be shy or hesitant.

Try to hire team members who will expand the business promise beyond you, not just replicate it on your behalf. It was Brian Tuckman in 1965 who first proposed the stages that groups need to go through in order to be a success. Consider these stages for getting a team to work well:

- ▶ Form – put the team together carefully
- ▶ Storm – collect ideas from every member
- ▶ Norm – watch it settle down and adjust if necessary
- ▶ Perform – enjoy the results

Draw it all together and make a plan. Give the team a purpose and a style. Find a way of articulating it to your team, make sure it reflects your personality, and tell them clearly what is expected of them. Then tell them what their specific personal action is to make the whole thing work. To do this you need to consider their individual qualities and work out how to work with them. Make sure you consider how you come across. Picture a person or customer you have met for the first time. Write down your first impressions and how they come across in a meeting. Now do the same exercise for yourself as though one of your team members is analyzing you. What are you really like? Which of the following are you? Child (poor little me); parent (bossy); or adult (confident, sensible, not all ego). This is a system that psychologists use to classify leadership skills at work. Consider your findings and adjust your behaviour if necessary. Part of doing this is to set a good example. Behave as you would want your team to. Be honest, enthusiastic, optimistic, resilient, and a good listener. Don't be a bully, or panic stricken. Manage your team with control and inspiration. Listen carefully and always make time for them. Never allow two people to do a job that one could do. If you want action, talk to them – don't issue written orders from on high.

Reward good things appropriately and develop a performance review system to keep everybody on track, but do add your own informal chats regularly. Pay attention to what they are going through, and try to make it fun to work in your team. When people aren't having any fun, they don't produce good work. Don't forget simple treats like chocolate and biscuits as well as the odd drink. But before you reward somebody, think clearly about why. What signals does it send to the rest? Can you spread the rewards around a bit? Reward staff that demonstrate a good aptitude for problem solving, innovation, decisive and confident action, smart work (not necessarily just busy work), quiet and effective behaviour, loyalty, teamwork and cooperation. Praise judiciously. There is nothing worse than a boss who relentlessly claims that everything and everyone is brilliant, when they clearly aren't. Share the credit whenever possible. It costs you nothing. As the old saying goes, the way to get things done is not to mind who gets the credit for doing them.

Try to delegate calmly and maturely. Do some of the nasty stuff yourself, and then delegate the rest to a team member. Remember that one person's drudgery can be another's enjoyment (or greater responsibility). Also delegate some of the nice things too. Let them know they are eminently capable of doing new tasks, but offer help if they need it. Share the responsibilities and let them enjoy it. Ask for consensus, but make the decisions. The buck stops with you. Relax and enjoy it.

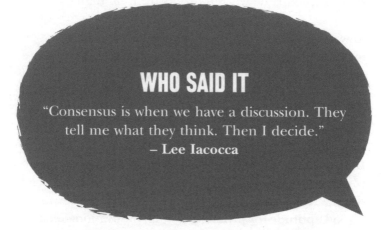

## WHO SAID IT

"Consensus is when we have a discussion. They tell me what they think. Then I decide."
– Lee Iacocca

# RECRUITING THE RIGHT PEOPLE AND KEEPING THEM MOTIVATED

Once you have decided on the shape of the team you need, you can set about recruiting. This is often easier said than done. Each role will involve different skills. If you require staff with specific skills, then these need to be explained and made plain in the job specification to avoid wasting time. General or non-trade-specific skills may be teachable quite quickly, which means you need to build training time into the early part of the job, or consider an assessment day before deciding who to hire. If soft, service-type skills are the main thing, then you are more likely to have to rely on the vagaries of interviews

# WHO YOU NEED TO KNOW
*Larry Page and Sergei Brin*

Larry Page and Sergei Brin are the founders of Google. They are famous for allowing their staff to have 20% of their time off for 'goofing around', although the idea isn't as altruistic as it sounds since many of their most successful revenue-generating ideas have been invented during such free time.

Google began life in 1996 as a research project when Page and Brin were both PhD students at Stanford University in California. While conventional search engines ranked results by counting how many times the search terms appeared on the page, the two theorized about a better system that analyzed the relationships between websites. They called this new technology PageRank, where a website's relevance was determined by the number of pages, and the importance of those pages, that linked back to the original site.

The Google domain name was registered in 1997 and the business was set up in a friend's garage in Menlo Park, California. The company's mission from the outset was 'to organize the world's information and make it universally accessible and useful', but its unofficial slogan – coined by engineer Paul Buchheit – is 'Don't be evil'. This attitude has served them well on the road to becoming one of the most successful businesses in the world.

Specifically, Google treats its staff as 'knowledge workers', who are paid to be effective, not to work 9 to 5. They hire by committee, and virtually every person who interviews talks to at least half-a-dozen interviewers, drawn from management and potential colleagues. Everyone's opinion counts. Their ideas mailing list is a companywide suggestion box where people can post ideas ranging from parking procedures to the next killer app. The software allows for everyone to comment on and rate ideas, permitting the best ideas to percolate to the top. Every Friday there is an all-hands assembly with announcements, introductions and questions and answers, which allows management to stay in touch with what staff are thinking and vice versa.

to make your decision. Interviewing is imperfect in giving an accurate view of what someone will be like at a job, but in many instances it is the only choice employers have.

Once you have met a candidate you think fits the bill, do take the time to make enquiries via references provided by previous employers. Although these are requested and provided at most interviews, it is surprising how few prospective employers take the time to follow them up. If you are still uncertain, consider a trial period in which either side can say that they don't think it is working out. Particularly in the early days, it is important to have open lines of communication so that both sides can make it clear how things are going. Talk to your staff and find out if they feel they are making a difference, if they are learning anything, and whether they are enjoying themselves. Sometimes being very busy stops you taking the time, but there are lots of ways to build team morale when things are manic. Try to deal with problems by making them impersonal. To a large degree you can create your own luck by having lots of ideas and enacting them as fast as possible. Every now and then, reflect on the achievements of the team and tell them what they are. Don't dwell on misfortunes or label yourself or the team as unlucky. Recognize the difference between bad luck and probability, because nothing goes smoothly all the time.

Every now and then take time out to go and congratulate a colleague for their good work. Be natural and offer to help. Take an interest in what is happening in their lives outside work. Try to learn from mistakes and share in success. Be as objective as you can about past performance – if things weren't great, say so. Good leaders regard everything as a learning experience, and are not ashamed or frightened to admit deficiencies. They harness the findings as a team, share the responsibility, avoid defensiveness, and move on to the next thing better informed.

If something the team is working on is patently not going right, don't be scared to ditch an idea, service or product. If things go wrong, work out why and make changes. If things *are* great, work out why and spread the word to replicate success elsewhere. Think of things you can do differently to make work more enjoyable for you and your team. Create enforced thinking time so they can reflect on how things are going. Pay attention to the ideas and suggestions they come up with. Spend time simplifying things to make them shorter and less time-consuming. Don't just tell them what to do – help them to improve their efforts collectively. Often the combined thinking of the team is better than anything you could come up with on your own.

# HOW TO DEAL WITH PROBLEMS

Minimize politics and try to deal with problems fairly. Taking sides or trying to engineer staff into situations doesn't usually work. Team members who behave in this way are often divisive, so it is important to set an appropriate tone. Relax and let your confidence and experience speak for itself. Do you have politics in the team? If so, work out why and try to eliminate it. Identify any problem children in the team, and resolve issues as quickly as you can. If you have to take unpopular remedial action, do so swiftly and fairly. Don't make a drama out of it, and explain to the other team members what has happened and why you have done what you've done.

When problems with staff do arise, it is important to know how to conduct a proper review meeting or appraisal. In preparation, take time to consider whether there is likely to be a severe discrepancy between your view of the person and their performance, and the self-perception of the individual. This happens more often than you might think. Ask short, open-ended questions, and don't interrupt the answers.

> ▶ Ask if they are making a difference in their role
> ▶ Ask if they are learning anything new
> ▶ Ask if they are enjoying their role
> ▶ Ask if they are happy in themselves

If you don't think you are getting the whole story, ask simple questions to probe. Don't ask any loaded questions that are biased or merely reflect your side of the story. Don't insult the person by being late, or delaying the meeting, or being unprepared. Show as much interest in the review as the individual does, and remember that, to the individual, this could well be their most important meeting of the year. Be clear and calm through-out, and be receptive to new ideas – don't squash them on the spot. Instead, offer to go away and attend to issues. This shows authority and flexibility. If there is a nasty problem area, then don't be afraid to reconvene later when you've attended to it, or sought advice elsewhere. In any event, don't make promises on the spur of the moment that you can't keep.

One approach to keeping problems to a minimum is to only do business with people you like. This is quite a tricky area but it really is worth spending the time to work out how you feel about your business relationships. The principle can apply equally to your staff and your custom-ers. As the employer, you should have the final say on the nature of the team you hire. So try to make sure as far as possible that they reflect your style. With regard to customers, if you run a retail outlet then clearly you can't vet everybody with whom you have a transaction. But you can choose the nature of your suppliers and associates. And as you develop your own personal style, you will become better at working out what other people are like to deal with. Eventually, you should be in a position whereby it is you who chooses to do business with some-body, not the other way round.

Why is this important? Because ultimately, if you do not enjoy the company of the people with whom you have to interact, you will effectively have engineered a state of affairs in which you don't like what you do. This is a disaster for anyone who runs their own business. Indeed, the whole point of starting your own business is to design a set-up that suits your particular style. Of course, sometimes it takes a while for someone to show their true colours, and there will be times when somebody you really like lets you down. Unfortunately, there is nothing you can do about this, and it is undoubtedly true that any disappointments will be felt harder by you as an individual than by companies in the collective sense. However, in the long run, your judgement will improve with experience, and your goal should be only to do business with people that you like.

## WHO SAID IT

"The older I get, the more I admire and crave competence – just simple competence, in any field from adultery to zoology."
– H. L. Mencken

# SUSTAINING RELATIONSHIPS

Building a network of contacts will provide excellent moral support as well as potential business. You should network nonstop – this is a job that should never be finished. Running your own business is as much about relationships as it is about content or product. Concentrate hard on communication, particularly with partners and staff. Try to leave your ego at home – no one else is interested. Look for the best in people. Treat everyone with the same respect, and smile a lot. A crucial component of your business network should be others that have started their own business. They all go through what you go through, and there are few more unifying features than this one crucial bit of common ground. So whenever business owners meet, they usually end up with lots to discuss. The sort of stuff they talk about is often very wide-ranging, precisely because they are juggling all the work and personal issues that this book covers. This may sound self-evident, but consider the number of business meetings between those who work for large corporations that rarely get near to touching on their feelings or social lives – the things that matter to them most.

So the conversations between those who run their own businesses are very broad and have a tremendous capacity to generate genuine empathy. Put simply, you are very likely to sympathize with each other and to get on. That's a good basis for a relationship. You will both want to pay significant attention to what the other is good at, and what they enjoy doing. This makes sense because you are in the same boat and you might be able to help each other. That's a good equation in anyone's book. If this state of affairs is repeated over multiple conversations for a year or two, you are going to develop an extensive set of contacts with other business owners with whom you can swap experiences and other contacts.

Many small business owners use a mentor to provide helpful background support or 'air cover'. This could be a respected family member such as a parent, or an official business mentor, or even a non-Executive Director. Whatever their title or position, their role is to provide calm occasional advice, words of wisdom, and a steadying hand if things are veering off track. They also provide a valuable sounding board if there is an issue you cannot discuss with your own staff. Their views and experience are valuable whether they work in your sphere of business or not. Those who do similar work to you can compare specifics about your field, and they may be very useful to know about when it comes to referring surplus work. But those who do not work in your sector are equally fascinating to talk to. As well as all the general issues that confront those who work on their own, you may well find that it is their very lack of knowledge about your area that makes their comments all the more valuable. You have all heard people say 'I'm too close to it', so this type of encounter offers the equivalent of an objective commentator whose opinions are not biased by what they think they already know about your subject. This is also where social media, email, and online chat rooms come into their own. If you use them for this moral support purpose, you are using them well.

How would you feel if the phone rang and there was a business contact on the line offering you work? Not a full-time job, you understand, just a really decent piece of business of the type where you usually have to invest a lot of time to secure it. This time, the pre-sale work has all been done, and they are offering it to you because they can't do it themselves. There could be lots of reasons. They are too busy. They are going on holiday. They were asked about it, but it isn't precisely what they are best at. So they call to ask if you would be interested. It's a great feeling, and it happens when you have let others know what you do, and when you have offered to help them if they ever get stuck. It works both ways. You may well have been in the same position yourself and referred some work to them some time in the past. Whatever the reason, it is one of the most cost-effective calls you will ever receive.

This is a 'golden phone call', and they really can work in both directions. These calls move back and forth between well-connected people all the time. They come about because you have presented your skills well, been thoughtful in introducing contacts to each other, and often because you have already generated business for the person who is calling you now. Even better, these calls are completely free. They involve none of the usual investment of time and effort that most new business pursuits do. And once you have set the ball rolling, they start working their way back to you. Sometimes these interrelationships can progress a step further by turning into proper working alliances and subcontracting arrangements. Having an overflow facility for your business is good, and so is picking up work from contacts when you have not had to over-invest in securing it.

# WHO YOU NEED TO KNOW
## *Ricardo Semler*

Ricardo Semler is internationally famous for creating the world's most unusual workplace. His management philosophy of empowering employees and looking at corporate structures in new ways is a constant challenge to the ingrained models of the corporate pyramid.

At his company, Semco, workers choose their own bosses. Financial information is shared with everyone. A high percentage of the employees determine their own salaries and self-managed teams replace hierarchy and procedure. There are also always two spare seats kept free at every board meeting for any member of staff to attend. When there is an issue, one of Semler's favourite approaches is to do nothing on the grounds that common sense will eventually prevail.

He has appeared on television all over the world and has lectured to over 500 audiences. He has been chosen as a global leader by the World Economic Forum, *Fortune* magazine, and Dow Jones. Not all of his alternative approaches to dealing with people will suit everyone, but they are a stimulating counterpoint to most staid working practices.

151

# STAYING IN TOUCH

Enjoying the camaraderie of other companies is a smart way to stay in touch. Any company with two or more people in it will begin to develop its own culture. This usually happens the moment two people decide to take a break and go to the pub. By the time there is a full payroll, all sorts of social activities start to develop. Banter in reception. Jokes around the coffee machine. A quick drink after work. Sporting challenges. Mutual hobbies. The bigger the company, the more there is of it, so this will inevitably develop as your company grows. And chances are that many of your customers and suppliers are in a similar position, which means that there is a hybrid of business and social life waiting out there for you and your colleagues to join when you need it. There are probably hundreds of enjoyable opportunities lurking within many of your customer relationships, so it is your job to work out what type and frequency of interaction provides you with the right balance. Chances are that these social interactions will have a positive bonding effect on your customer relationships too.

Blurring the lines between work and social life is generally good, assuming that in the main you choose to do business with people that you like. Is it likely that your business could generate a lot of business out of social situations? Certainly. The old-fashioned lines of demarcation between work and play have become more blurred. We know that you can't permanently be in work mode, but equally you can't be in constant play mode either. What you can do is take a more relaxed view about whether you are 'on duty' or not. This does not cut only in favour of relaxing more. It also means that when you are socializing, you may equally be 'working'. The balance you create here is really important. It doesn't have to be arduous either way. That's why you need to have your antenna scanning for work opportunities, common areas, contacts, ideas, and so on, but all in a relaxed social context. Don't force it or get uptight. Keep it loose and stay open-minded. You really never do know when an amazing opportunity is lurking in the next enjoyable night out.

The owner-manager network can be viewed like an extended family. How often do you see the members of your family? The answer to this question varies enormously by individual. Some people live next door to their family members and see them all the time. Some have emigrated and are lucky to see them once a year. Somewhere in the middle lies a mixture of contact points and frequencies that the family members work out amongst themselves. You will know roughly how often you speak to your parents, siblings, grandparents, cousins, and so on, and in return, so will they. Your business contacts can be viewed in exactly the same way so that you can judge the appropriate frequency that suits the relationship. Once you have thought about this, you will have unwittingly designed a latticework of contact points. The family analogy may also help you to classify some of your contacts. Who are the 'must call once a week' customers? Who are the less well-known relations who are happy to chat once every few months? Once you get the hang of it, you can extend the metaphor from phone calls to meetings, anniversaries, parties – pretty much any inter-action that has a bearing on the business but that can spill into a social setting.

Bear in mind that, in the main, if you stay in touch, they will too. Although there are always some people in the world who never seem to return calls or invitations, most right-minded people do stay in touch. Once you get rolling with your 'keep in touch' programme, it will start to generate contacts in return without you actually doing anything. You will soon discover that you are not the sole initiator of an outbound contact programme. Don't forget that other people will be doing exactly the same thing. The number of people with whom you stay in touch, and the frequency with which you do so, is critical. You must not fritter away your energy by frequently con-tacting people who won't keep in touch with you in return. It's a waste of your time, and that ultimately means money. So it is important that you review regularly the people with whom you stay in touch, and whether it is worth your while. At the beginning, you need to develop an initial pool of contacts, and of course until you have attempted to stay in touch with someone for a reasonable period, you won't know what their track record is in this regard. But as soon as you realize that they never really bother to stay in touch and so do not represent any kind of business opportunity, then you need seriously to consider whether they should be dropped from your Contact List.

Perhaps not surprisingly, people can be one of the hardest issues you have to cope with. You have to love what you do and stay true to it so as to send out the right consistent message to the people with whom you interact. Equally, there are some people it's just not worth trying with, so don't be afraid to move on from something if it is not working. Be with the people you enjoy being with as much as possible, and never be afraid to ask advice from someone you admire. Treat everybody as you would expect to be treated yourself. Believe in what you are doing and at the same time listen to healthy criticism. Forge a team that you believe can do the job and work hard at keeping them motivated. Deal with problems fast and fairly, and sustain your relationships with care and attention.

## WHAT YOU NEED TO READ

▶ *Leadership for Dummies* by Marshall Loeb and Stephen Kindel (John Wiley and Sons Ltd) synthesizes much of what it takes to deal with people, stressing in particular how successful business leaders need to be prepared to take on risk, change and ambiguity.

▶ *www.ezinearticles.com* contains a range of people management articles, including Eight Essential People Skills.

▶ *www.lifecoachexpert.co.uk* has a whole library of case studies and advice for developing Effective Leadership and People Management Skills.

▶ *The Seven-Day Weekend* by Ricardo Semler (Century) explains his unusual approach to dealing with people in the work place, and many of his ideas can be put into practice straightaway.

▶ Rob Goffee and Gareth Jones have produced several books on leadership. *Why Should Anyone Be Led By You?* (Harvard Business School Press) asks a very fair question and stresses that you have to earn the respect of those that work for you. Another book, *Clever* (Harvard Business School Press), deals specifically with leading very intelligent and highly creative people.

# IF YOU ONLY REMEMBER ONE THING

Consider carefully the people you need, and shape your team. Work hard to inspire those around you, and treat them as you would wish to be treated yourself.

# CHAPTER 7

# GROWTH AND DURABILITY

## WHAT IT'S ALL ABOUT ➡

- ▶ Pros and cons of growth
- ▶ Analyze your products and services
- ▶ Keeping things varied
- ▶ Dealing with setbacks

In general, growth is a good thing, but for the small business owner it is important not to see it as an end in its own right. Continual growth is more likely to be required by large public companies with investors and shareholders hungrily pushing for their dividends and returns. In the rather more humble world of starting and running your own business, however, this may be less important. Obviously when you start, you start from scratch, and so year one will always involve growth. But if you succeed your desired size and state fairly soon, say in the first year, then further growth may not be what you want thereafter. For example, if you successfully establish a coffee shop with four staff, then you might not want to open a second one. So it is important to view growth in its broadest context so that you can pursue an appropriate, manageable rate of it. This is a quite separate point from durability. All businesses should aspire to durability.

# THE PROS AND CONS OF GROWTH

Sometimes starting is the easy bit. After the initial excitement there are new challenges, and getting bored or stagnating in year two is one of them. You need a view on what type of growth is good for your business, and how you are going to remain enthusiastic about it. As a starting point, it is good to ask whether growth is always a good thing. Although the answer sounds obvious, it may not be as simple as it first appears. For some businesses, reaching a certain level and staying there might be more desirable than growth for the sake of it. Straightforward survival might even be acceptable for many. Growth might be necessary, or desirable, but it certainly brings with it many issues.

To stay as you are is impossible in the strictest sense, because there will always be something about your business that is changing, even if the essential shape of it is the same, and sales are the same as last year. Momentum is important but size in itself is not. Many people who start a business have a certain shape in mind, and if they achieve it within the first year or two, then maintaining that will be the goal, not world domination. Nevertheless, many entrepreneurs claim that it is important to adopt a mentality of growth, even if growth is not the main objective. Most agree that there is good growth and bad growth. Good growth is planned, expected, and comes judiciously. The business gears up appropriately. Resources and staff come along on the journey in a reasonably orderly way, and methodical forward motion keeps everyone happy. The chances of this happening smoothly are, of course, quite low. Most businesses experience lurches in fortunes to which they have to adjust. Growth is good as long as it is profitable. If growth merely lowers the margin then the business may superficially appear to be in great shape when in fact it is heading for a loss, albeit from a bigger base. As such, it is critical to differentiate between higher turnover and better margin. Higher turnover is good if it brings with it no loss of quality and no margin reduction (even better if the margin rises). Higher turnover with a slightly lower margin may just be acceptable, but any significant margin reduction is not desirable. As the old saying goes, turnover is vanity, profit is sanity.

Bad growth is doing things for the wrong reasons. Rapid growth can endanger quality and reputation. Standards can slip if a company pursues money just for the sake of it. Getting the order out of the door at breakneck speed simply to rush into the next customer's demands may build a business in the short term but is unlikely to be sustainable. It could simply generate a misleading spurt of activity and build up problems for later. It is important to make sure that quality of service and product is maintained. Of course growth usually involves making a lot of mistakes. This is understandable and perfectly fine as long as lessons are genuinely learned. If the mistakes are ignored and simply repeated, then no progress is made. Knowing when to turn down business is an important skill to develop. Natural instinct suggests that you should accept all business that is offered, but this may be a mistake. Customers that prove problematic can ruin the business you have carefully built up. This could be because they are demanding lower prices, because they are unpleasant to deal with, or just because they unwittingly force you into areas that you didn't originally have in mind. Remember that a principle isn't a principle until it costs you money

So be careful to manage, control and plan your growth as far as you possibly can. It's your business, so you reserve the right to dictate how it develops. Do not pursue growth for growth's sake. Instead, devise your vision for what the business should do, and then the growth will follow. Equally, do not compromise or dilute what you set out to achieve in the first place, or what your customers consistently tell you that they like. Many businesses have veered off by not 'sticking to the knitting'.

# WHO SAID IT

"Every man takes the limits of his own field of vision for the limits of the world."
– **Schopenhauer**

# ANALYZE YOUR PRODUCTS AND SERVICES

Imagine your business as a series of rivers and dams. These will be areas where everything is flowing well, or where there are frequent blockages that prevent you from conducting your business properly. The first step is to ask some questions and write down the answers. Start with the good stuff:

► Where are the rivers?
► How many of them are there?
► How large?
► How small?

Then repeat the process for the not-so-good things. Which do you have more of – rivers or dams? This exercise should allow you to see at a glance what works in your business, and what doesn't. It will also reveal straight away whether the business has more good things going on than bad, or vice versa. Don't panic if there seem to be way more dams than rivers. Your next step should be to initiate more rivers and unblock the dams as fast as possible.

Ballistics is the study of the flight dynamics of projectiles: the interaction of the forces of propulsion, projectile aerodynamics, atmospheric resistance and gravity. These five areas provide a useful analogy for working out why things are happening in your business:

► Projectiles: who, or what, is heading where?
► Propulsion forces: who, or what, is making them do that?
► Aerodynamics: who, or what, has good momentum behind it?
► Resistance: who, or what, is resisting forward motion?
► Gravity: is there anything structural that anchors any of this?

You can now review the rivers and dams information through the eyes of the ballistics categories. Use the questions associated with each component to try to unravel how something might be resolved. For example, does a resistance question help solve an issue? Does the gravity of the business explain why something is as it is? Does a propulsion force provide a clue as to how to fix a dam? The sequence of questions can be repeated for each type of motion. What type of motion are we dealing with here? Who, or what, is heading where? Is that good or bad? If it's good, how can it be replicated elsewhere? If it's bad, how can it be fixed?

If you work in a highly technical business area and have specialist staff, you may need to involve them in this process. Their knowledge of the technical detail may be able to answer some of the more tricky questions, and there is no point in generating scores of questions that you cannot personally answer. Far better to embark on the process with an approximate idea of what you think might emerge, and have the necessary people on hand to help you out. Diving into any wide-ranging thought process without decent preparation is also inadvisable. If you embark on it with only one angle, you may only generate the one solution, and it will probably be the same as everything you have come up with before. Most issues have multiple possible solutions, so you need to stay open-minded as to what these might be. By the end of this exercise you should have a comprehensive review of your products and services, and an action plan of what to do next.

A word of warning about the positive things that fall into the rivers category: do not be tempted to claim that these things were wonderfully devised and thought through if, in truth, they were actually a fluke. Only you know the reality of this. If you allow this to happen, then you will assume that their success can be replicated if you repeat the process, which may not be the case. So when looking back at successes in your business and looking for inspiration, always admit if something happened by chance. Far too many people (and businesses) rewrite history to claim that a random success was carefully thought through when many are not.

# WHO YOU NEED TO KNOW
### *Jim Collins*

Jim Collins is a student and teacher of enduring great companies – how they grow, how they attain superior performance and how good companies can become great companies. He is the co-author of *Built To Last* (the successful habits of visionary companies) and the author of *Good To Great* (why some companies make the leap and others don't). He jettisoned a traditional academic career in 1995 and now works from his management laboratory in Boulder, Colorado.

In 1994 *Built To Last* conducted a marathon six-year research study to examine companies from their conception, in some cases 100 years before, to their current position. All had outperformed the stock market by a factor of fifteen, and were used as the bedrock of a think piece about how companies could create and sustain enduring success. It was a monster that spawned sales over a million, and probably as many boardroom conversations.

By 2001, *Good To Great* embarked on another mammoth research study (five years this time) to work out how companies can migrate from being merely good to being great. But by the time he had finished, he wondered whether it should in fact have been the prequel to *Built To Last* rather than the sequel. In other words, first you raise your company standards from good to great, and then the resulting organization will truly be built to last. Strange to conclude then, that perhaps he should have done it the other way round.

If one were to try to summarize his findings over both studies, it would be to ignore charismatic leaders, complex strategies and the competition – if you want enduring success, concentrate on having a common sense of purpose.

# KEEPING THINGS VARIED

To run a successful business you need to stay sane and relentlessly enthusiastic. The definition of sanity is 'the state of having a normal healthy mind' or 'good sense and soundness of judgement', so we are describing the condition of a rational person who feels well balanced and reasonably calm. Many aspects of modern life would appear to be designed to unhinge us at every opportunity, and the pressures of any breadwinner in today's society are well documented. So it is important that you engineer a set-up that keeps you as calm as possible. Equally, enthusiasm is an absolutely fundamental prerequisite of someone who runs a business. Nobody else is going to generate business for you. No one else is going to be enthusiastic on your behalf. The job falls to you. People don't usually want to do business with someone who lacks enthusiasm, so one way or another you need to find a way of having an endless supply of the stuff. Keep lots of variety in what you do to stay fresh. Get keyed up for phone calls and meetings, and try to be in a good mood before you do them. Change things if you don't find them interesting. And take a sensible amount of time off so that you can return to your work energetically.

The net effect for your customers should be that your enthusiasm appears to be relentless even though, of course, it is impossible for any person to be in that state as a permanent condition. A vital part of this is taking the right amount of time off work. How many times have you heard a self-employed person say that they haven't had a holiday for ages? Even if they have arranged it and left the country, they still keep worrying about the business when they are lying on a beach somewhere. This is a poor formula that usually leads to some form of meltdown, with both the business and the individual inevitably suffering.

One helpful trick is to build time off into your plan for the year. Try not to do it on the fly halfway through. If you do it ad hoc like this, there is a very strong chance that the break that you do go for won't really do the trick. You will almost certainly have compromised on one aspect or another, and this does not befit the reward that you have earned. So look at the year and ask yourself these sorts of questions:

- ▶ When are the best times of year to be away?
- ▶ Will you take one large chunk or several smaller bits?
- ▶ Do you need a sabbatical?
- ▶ If so, how would you arrange it?
- ▶ Could you plan to work a 10-month year instead of 12?
- ▶ Where do you want to go?
- ▶ In what sort of style?
- ▶ With anyone else or on your own?
- ▶ What sort of research do you need to do before you can answer some of these questions?

When you take time off, try to be genuinely unavailable. There is little point in taking a break if you spend a vast amount of it checking messages on your mobile phone or logging on to your e-mail system. Be sure to put the measures in place to explain why you are not around before you make yourself unavailable. Also don't forget that corporate time moves differently to normal time, so many of your customers may not even notice that you have gone away anyway.

Try to follow these simple steps to taking time off and being *genuinely* unavailable. Put your mobile phone in a drawer and don't take it with you. If you must, then limit the times per day that you turn it on. Do not visit an internet café unless you have a burning need to contact a loved one. Do not take any work material with you at all. Change the messages on your phones to explain what is going on. Set up an auto response on your e-mail to do the same. Tell your customers a long way in advance that you will not be available (in certain types of work, this may even mean that you actually receive more work before you go so that their needs are covered whilst you are away). All in all, this approach works well. There will of course be some lines of work where you really do need to be contactable, but you can judge the level of that for yourself. If you apply even a few of these disciplines, you will stand a better chance of having a decent break, and that will be in everybody's interests.

# WHO YOU NEED TO KNOW
## *Lakshmi Mittal*

Lakshmi Mittal is an Indian national, steel tycoon and the chairman and Chief Executive of ArcelorMittal, the world's largest steelmaking company. Depending on which survey you read, he is the richest man in Europe and the fifth richest in the world, with a personal wealth of £19 billion. The *Financial Times* named him Person of the Year in 2006, and in 2007 he was named one of the 100 Most Influential People by *Time* magazine. He is also reputed to be the 44th most powerful person in the world, and one in every five cars in the world is made up of the steel materials of his empire. On the social front, his daughter's marriage was the most expensive in the recorded history of the world.

He started his career working in the family's steelmaking business in India, and in 1976 he set out to establish its international division, beginning with the buying of a run-down plant in Indonesia. As a result of differences with his family, he branched out on his own and he has been responsible for extraordinary growth ever since.

Arcelor Mittal is now a global steel producer with operations in 14 countries. He pioneered the development of integrated mini-mills and the use of direct reduced iron or DRI as a scrap substitute for steelmaking, and led the consolidation process of the steel industry. Arcelor Mittal is now the largest steelmaker in the world, with shipments of 42.1 million tons of steel and profits in the billions. This success did not happen overnight. Four decades of growth are testament to the durability of his vision and the company that brought it to life.

# WHO SAID IT

"The reasonable man adapts himself to the world; the unreasonable one persists in trying to adapt the world to himself. Therefore all progress depends on the unreasonable man."
– George Bernard Shaw

# DEALING WITH SETBACKS

Setbacks are an inevitable part of business life, but small businesses should not feel that they are at the mercy of larger ones. If, on reflection, you feel that your business is being too servile, under-charging, over-delivering and generally being too subservient, then it is time to change something. Fear often prevents businesses from confronting customers who mistreat them, because they think they will lose the business, that they will never replace the income, or that the customer will never change their approach. The outcome is rarely as disastrous as was originally feared and it is undoubtedly better to 'die standing up than to live on your knees'. Sometimes, bullying customers do listen to comment and try to change their approach. Even if things can't be reconciled and their custom moves on, many businesses find this quite liberating because it allows them to reinvent themselves in another area with other customers.

Setbacks and mistakes are rife in business. It can be very cathartic to come clean about your business disasters. It is all about learning and being human. We all make mistakes, and when we have made enough, they call it experience. For example, some people have terrible trouble with their selection of business partner. They originally get together because they think they will make a good team, or that the other person will compensate for skills that they don't have, but after a while it can go wrong. The most commonly stated gripes are unclear roles, lack of communication, or changing opinions. So if you have a business partner, one key to durability is to talk frequently and make it clear what you want. On the personal front, all sorts of trouble can brew. Business owners talk of almost burning out, not looking after their personal relationships, and many other problems. This is a highly personal area, and it is important to pay attention to yourself, and those who care about you, so that the business doesn't take over your life.

Everyone, but everyone, has money troubles. These include, in no particular order, insufficient financial systems, spending beyond their means, not seeking outside investment, under-pricing (and then not being able to raise prices), and not chasing outstanding money quickly enough. The trick is to identify these issues early and do something swiftly. Once you have rectified the problem, you can laugh about it later, or reflect on it ruefully. But make sure that you act fast enough to stop the business going under.

When it comes to not having enough income, there are two main mistakes that businesses make:

1. Not doing enough business development when they are busy
2. Expending too much time, energy and emotion on tactical new business efforts

Number one is a common problem. Always try to make time for developing your business even when you are right in the middle of coping with what you already have. If you become over-dependent on one or two sources of business, you might as well work for a corporation, and if that business suddenly goes away you will have no pipeline to fall back on. Losing a big or long-standing customer can be a serious blow, but it shouldn't be a surprise, nor should it be the end of your business. Customers move all the time, and the sooner you acknowledge it, the better. Allocating separate specific time for meeting potential customers and staying in the swing is vital. Equally though, you shouldn't expend too much effort on scores of little new business leads that are highly time-consuming but very tactical. A typical example of this is companies who draw up no plan of their own and so spend the whole time reacting to inbound enquiries that may or may not suit their needs.

One final point on growth and durability: If you find your business stalling, do stop and ask yourself this fundamental question – what was the original idea? It could refer to a number of things – why you set the business up in the first place, what the vision or purpose of your company is, why you bother to come to work in the morning – anything that is crucial to the matter in hand. The original idea always lies at the heart of what is important. So remind yourself what it was in the first place, and use that as an anchor point to rededicate yourself and your staff to the essence of what you are trying to do. This will help to cement your purpose and provide a clear platform for growth.

# WHAT YOU NEED TO READ

▶ *Why Entrepreneurs Should Eat Bananas* by Simon Tupman (Cyan Books) contains 101 inspirational ideas for growing your business and yourself. You can either use it to reinvigorate your company or to provide a fillip to your own attitude.

▶ *The Entrepreneur's Book of Checklists* by Robert Ashton (Prentice Hall) has 100 tips to help you grow your business.

▶ *www.growthbusiness.co.uk* contains a wealth of material on business development, including management articles, analysis and expert business insight.

▶ Bo Burlingham's book *Small Giants* (Penguin) explains that bigger is not necessarily better. He analyzes fourteen private companies that chose a different path to success: rejecting the pressure of endless growth, and instead concentrating on being the best at what they do, creating a stimulating place to work, and making important contributions to their communities.

- *Built To Last* and *Good To Great* by Jim Collins (Random House) explain the successful habits of visionary companies. Looking at these attributes and how they are sustained over time could provide useful clues that you can apply to your business.

- John Kay's *Obliquity* (Profile Books) explains why our goals are best achieved indirectly. In other words, if you try too hard to analyze something in your business, you may over-think it. It contains different ways of looking at issues.

- Simon Waldman's *Creative Disruption* (Prentice Hall) explains what you need to do to shake up your business in a digital world: transform the core, find big adjacencies, and innovate at the edges. If your business needs significant modernization, this is the place to start.

# IF YOU ONLY REMEMBER ONE THING

You need a view on whether growth is good for your business, and if so, what type. Remaining enthusiastic about it is most likely the key to durability.

# CHAPTER 8

# LIFESTYLE MATTERS

## WHAT IT'S ALL ABOUT

- ▶ You are the company culture
- ▶ Getting your attitude right
- ▶ Lifestyle and build-to-sell questions
- ▶ Why Plan B is often better than Plan A
- ▶ Take the issues seriously, but not yourself

In many small businesses, the lifestyle of the owner is indivisible from the nature of the company. It makes sense to set up a business whose style reflects your own, so it is important to keep tabs on whether this is truly the case, or whether the two have drifted apart. It starts by understanding the link between your own style and that of the business you run. Running a lifestyle business is perfectly fine, but it is quite different from building a business with the intention of selling it. Understanding the difference between the two approaches, and thinking it through before setting up the wrong shape of company, is important. Your business needs to suit your style whether you are using it to sustain a lifestyle or heading for a sale. The tone you set will be crucial.

# WHO SAID IT

"Be yourself; everyone else is already taken."
– Oscar Wilde

# YOU ARE THE COMPANY CULTURE

You are the company culture. Making your business fit your style is important for your long-term happiness and business success. You need to work this out before you unintentionally create a business that doesn't really suit you. Take a sheet of paper and write the question *What am I like?* at the top. Take ten minutes or so to write down your thoughts. This is supposed to be an honest assessment of how you come across. You can produce a series of notes, or a flow of observations, as long as it is what you genuinely think you are like. If relevant, you can highlight distinctions between how you think you come across, and how you really feel. If you have trouble doing this, try imagining how someone might describe you if they met you for the first time, or how you would describe yourself to someone you have never met. Many people have never answered this question of themselves before. Take your time and be brutally honest. This could reveal what you might want to change.

The next step is to define your style. Take another ten minutes to answer these questions:

▶ Who or what is your favourite person or team?
▶ What qualities make them so good?
▶ How can those qualities inspire your approach?

Everybody has a style, but they may never have paused to consider what it is. Now is the time to do it. Your personal style should dovetail perfectly with that of your business. If not, you may wish to adjust one or the other. Your business should be a conduit for your personal aspirations. You can't reconcile the two unless you know what you really want. So make sure you know, and then you can do something about it. Take another blank piece of paper and write at the top of it *I pledge*. Now write down what you are going to do differently from now on in order to achieve what you want. If you can't articulate it in your own words, answer these three questions:

▶ How exactly am I going to get where I want to be?
▶ Do I need help and, if so, from whom?
▶ By when will I achieve this?

Write down your pledge. This could be to yourself, your business, your family or friends. Writing something down and pinning it on the wall has a polarizing effect. Live with your pledge and see if you can live up to it.

# GETTING YOUR ATTITUDE RIGHT

Having a positive attitude is an important attribute. Try not to distinguish between nice and nasty things to do. It is human nature to say 'I love doing x' and 'I hate doing y'. Now that you are your own boss, you need to stop making the distinction between the two. Why? Because it was your decision to go it alone, and whatever needs doing has to be done and is ultimately entirely for your own personal benefit. Even if the task is working out how much tax to pay, it is worth doing well because if you don't, you may be the one to lose out. It is also inaccurate to presuppose that something you expect to be nasty will actually turn out to be so. In reality, the outcome of a situation that you are anxious about is frequently the opposite of what you expect it to be. This may sound contradictory but it is actually true. For instance, can you imagine how you might have a better meeting firing someone than giving them a pay rise? Have a look at these two examples.

> Employer: *I'm very sorry but after a lot of discussion and anxiety I'm afraid we can't keep you in this job any longer.*
>
> Employee: *I can't say I'm surprised. I haven't been coping very well and I haven't been happy. I was thinking of going travelling instead.*

This is proof that nasty things can turn out to be nice. Alternatively:

> Employer: *I am pleased to tell you that we have agreed a £3,000 pay rise for you.*
>
> Employee: *I'm really disappointed. I was expecting a minimum of £5,000.*

This is proof that nice things can turn out to be nasty. So, that supposedly nasty cold call looming on your checklist might well be the very thing that makes you most happy this month. Chances are, if you try to guess the outcome of something, you'll be wrong as often as you are right. So do not be tempted to second-guess outcomes in business. If in doubt, do the worst first and get it over with.

Reminding yourself of all the positive things you have done is a good way to stay positive. Many business owners suffer from some form of self-doubt. You may not have colleagues congratulating you on a job well done, so you need to generate your own humble form of self-congratulation. Consider these ideas for reminding yourself that you are actually pretty good at what you do and that you deserve a pat on the back:

▶ Write down your income
▶ Write down your profit
▶ Say out loud: 'I am still in business'
▶ Choose which recent business transaction was your favourite
▶ Ask a customer if they will write a reference for you
▶ Invent an ingenious plan for the near future
▶ Calculate whether you can afford a holiday soon
▶ Book a holiday
▶ If you have rivals, consider whether they are doing as well as you

Remember this straightforward maxim: everything you achieve, you have done yourself. Staying positive is healthy for you and all those around you. Equally, moaning is an unattractive feature of any personality, and is destructive for business morale. Try to stick to a 'No moaning' credo, and never be tempted to join in with a customer or colleague who is moaning. You can sympathize briefly, but then it is your job to suggest ways in which you can make things better. Work is called work because it involves effort. You get paid for what you put in. Remind yourself of this regularly and, if you ever catch yourself having a moan, nip it in the bud early.

# REWARDING YOURSELF

When your business makes some progress or reaches an important milestone, it is really important to reward yourself (and your staff) appropriately. The word 'reward' has many connotations, but it could mean something fairly modest. Small gestures that give a positive sense of pride in tasks well done can be just as useful as expensive or lavish ones. There are lots of different ways of rewarding yourself. Usually the scale of the reward should match the significance of the achievement. An hour away from the desk with a cappuccino and a Danish pastry might be triggered by the successful completion of your quarterly VAT return. Clearing everything on your checklist might justify a pint or two of premium lager. High praise from a customer might suggest an afternoon off to visit an art gallery. A significant new contract? Perhaps a slap-up meal with your partner and family. And a healthy profit for the year almost certainly means a well-deserved dividend.

Clearly, the first reward might cost a few pounds and the final one many thousands. An ability to reward yourself appropriately is a critical part of retaining your sanity when you work for yourself. Many business owners are working so hard that they never stop to appreciate what they have achieved. This rather defeats the object of setting it up in the first place. Try writing your own list. Start with an achievement column, taking little examples first that crop up frequently in your working day or week. Then move on to more significant monthly or annual milestones. Then dream up some suitable rewards to match each piece of progress. If you like what you have come up with, then put reminders in your diary for the long-term ones. These will turn into pleasant moments somewhere in the future, and play a part in generating a sense of momentum.

Self-reward is closely linked to daily reinvention, and that means not getting stuck in a rut. Keep things varied. Always be on the lookout for opportunities to do the unexpected and the new. Change as much as is appropriate as often as possible. Look for ways to be creative all the time. If everything has been the same for ages, then it is important to do something about it. Change not only keeps you stimulated, but it is usually good for customers too. You are less likely to be caught on the hop by the competition, and new ideas often capture the imagination of your customers, or help you to attract new ones.

As a quick method for stopping you or your business being stuck in a rut, take a piece of paper and write down the main things that your business does. Use a simple scoring system to rate your activities, services and products:

1. Absolutely hate it
2. Don't enjoy it
3. Boring but tolerable
4. Quite like it
5. Absolutely love it

Score each area of business based on your enjoyment. As you can see, the higher the score, the more satisfied you should be. The assumption here is that your enjoyment level will be closely correlated with the degree of sameness of your work and, to a degree, the length of time you have been doing it. Of course it is possible that you have been doing the same thing for years and you still love it – in which case, that is fine. More likely though, variety will increase enjoyment. Every now and again, ask yourself some searching questions. Is that the same as it has always been? Are you stimulated by it? Are you bored? Always change before your lack of enthusiasm seeps into your working day and becomes apparent to your customers. This process should also be conducted regularly with your staff, to make sure that they are not losing enthusiasm. In the main, the durability of your business is likely to be strongly correlated with the levels of passion and energy shown by you and your team.

## WHO YOU NEED TO KNOW

*Richard Branson*

In 1966, Richard Branson launched his first successful business – a magazine called *Student*. By 1970, he had started selling records by mail order, which led to the opening of his first record shop on Oxford Street in 1971. The Virgin Records label was launched two years later in 1973. The subsequent decades saw the company's business ventures grow significantly and it is now one of the most successful businesses in the world.

Throughout, however, Richard Branson has demonstrated a great knack for applying his personal style to a bewildering array of business sectors. The group's company statement gives an excellent insight into their strategy on expansion and diversity:

"Contrary to what some people may think, our constantly expanding and eclectic empire is neither random nor reckless. Each successive venture demonstrates our devotion to picking the right market and the right opportunity. When we start a new venture, we base it on hard research and analysis. We ask fundamental questions: is this an opportunity for restructuring a market and creating competitive advantage? Is the customer confused or badly served? Is this an opportunity for building the Virgin Brand? Can we add value?"

Branson's personal values shine through in all of this. He believes that if you have faith in yourself, anything can be done. He recommends that you live life to the full and never give up – wise words indeed for those starting businesses.

# LIFESTYLE AND BUILD-TO-SELL QUESTIONS

There are some crucial questions you really need to grapple with in order to reconcile your lifestyle with your ambitions for your business. It is important to consider these at the beginning, because it will have a significant bearing on how you run the company. If you think that you will eventually want to sell your business, you need to answer five questions:

1. If you want to sell, who will buy?
2. What exactly will they be buying?
3. What price do you want?
4. How will you justify the price?
5. Will you be able to work for someone else during the earn-out period?

## 1. If you want to sell, who will buy?

Many people intend to sell their business but fail to address this question. They think that building a business with an income base will automatically appeal to some unknown potential buyer at some point in the future, but it may not. Thousands of businesses have a substantial income base and yet significant problems. These can include:

▶ The customers could disappear any minute
▶ The business doesn't make a big enough profit
▶ The business doesn't make a regular profit
▶ The business isn't very well run
▶ The business will be ineffective without you personally
▶ The market has moved on by the time you want to sell

Any accountant or potential purchaser will spot these holes very quickly. Some business owners think that someone will buy because lots of other similar companies have been bought in their market recently. This could be a self-deception – it may simply mean that the market is saturated and that the buying spree has finished. Only three per cent of UK businesses make it to 100 employees, so the chances of arriving at a saleable endgame are quite low. You need to review your market and work out who the possible purchasers are before you build a company that fits the needs of the potential purchaser. Are there acquisitive holding companies operating in your sector? Are there venture capitalists hovering around? Are there rivals who are expanding and might want to swallow you up to reduce their competition? Will they still be around and interested when you have built something worth buying? You need to think about all this carefully.

Take the time to write down all the possible acquirers of your business. If there are ten, then consider whether they will have the time, money or inclination to suit your needs. Then consider whether the timing you desire is likely to suit them. What if they go out of business or change their priorities before the proposed sale? Think hard. This will probably eliminate some of the candidates. If there are only a handful of names on the list, your chances are slim. If there is only one, it may well not happen. And if there are none, then building to sell may be an unrealizable ambition.

## 2. What exactly will they be buying?

Some business owners aim to sell their business when in truth there isn't actually anything to buy. This sounds strange, but the business world is full of hubris that can blur judgement. You only have to look at Enron to see that. The fact of the matter is, someone will only buy your business if it will make them money. As far as the purchaser is concerned, the principle is incredibly simple: show me your accounts and I will work out whether I can make money out of buying your business.

## 3. What price do you want?

Of those business owners who say that they will sell their business one day, many haven't actually identified a price, and those that have often have an unrealistically inflated price in mind. It is a proven fact that we all value our own possessions more highly than anyone else. Another common flaw is failing to realize what sacrifices will need to be made in order to generate a suitable sale price. Take tax, for example. Those who have sold their business for £1 million do not necessarily receive the whole amount in the way that they might imply in the pub. They will have to give 20–40% to the taxman. So that's £600,000–800,000. The payments may be staged, probably over three years or more. The last payment might be based on performance, so if the company hasn't performed that well in the final stage, which often happens, then the price will come down even further. So the so-called millionaire may only have a fraction of that in their pocket – the same amount, quite possibly, as the person who hasn't sold their business.

## 4. How will you justify the price?

You need to be able to justify the sale price you have in mind. The potential purchaser will view it as a set of historical accounts, and then project what they can earn in the future. Although there are occasional instances of businesses selling in the first few years, this is very unusual. It is reasonable to regard five years as the minimum time period that the accountants will want to look at to prove that your business is worth buying – and it might be ten years, depending on the nature of your market. They will want to see a minimum of the last three years showing healthy profit. They will want assurances that this is a sustainable position that won't fall away if they buy. They will calculate a multiple of these profits to generate a possible price. This will most likely ensure that they get their money back within three years and start making a healthy profit thereafter.

## 5. Will you be able to work for someone else during the earn-out period?

When someone has agreed to buy your business, they are unlikely to let you leave straight away. Many businesses are people businesses, and the purchasers won't want the founder leaving immediately and risking major customers walking out. Instead, they may tie you in for an earn-out period, typically three years, to protect their investment. So you have to ask yourself something important: after working for myself for many years, could I suddenly work for someone else? Think hard before you decide that you are building your business to sell.

Alternatively, if you suspect that you might want to run a lifestyle business, there are four crucial questions you need to consider:

1. What type of lifestyle?
2. How much time off do I want?
3. Who else is involved?
4. What happens if I get ill?

# 1. What type of lifestyle?

A lifestyle business fits around whatever style of life you want. Most of us are happy with a reasonably decent living and some security for the people we love. We need enough to survive, something for retirement, and hopefully some surplus to have a pleasant time on the way. By all means design a plan that makes you a fortune, but don't assume it will happen as a matter of course. A subsistence business is perfectly acceptable as long as the owner doesn't treat it as a lifestyle business. In other words, it is not until the business is making a decent surplus over a sustained period that it can be classified as a fully-fledged lifestyle business. As a rough guide, that would be a 30% profit or more over three years.

## 2. How much time off do I want?

A common mistake when projecting annual income is to assume that you will be working every hour of the day, night, week, month, or year. You won't. It may feel like it at the beginning, and you may be fantastically hard working. But one day you will fall over, exhausted or ill, which is no way to plan a business. So you need to plan the rest periods in from the beginning. Work out when your customers are less active, and see if you can go away then. Is your business seasonal? There's no point in working when there's no one to do business with. Do you have hobbies? Then go away when the weather suits best. Do you have family? Then build in school half terms or whatever suits the pattern. This is absolutely essential for sole traders, because if you are shattered, then the business might be too.

## 3. Who else is involved?

Another crucial question is: who else is involved? This could apply to anyone else whose quality of life could be affected by the manner in which you succeed or fail when running your business. If the answer is no one, then there is certainly less pressure. In theory you can go bankrupt, scrape by on very little, or disappear for months on end, as long as the income is acceptable to you. That's pretty rare though, because most of us have someone that matters. Husbands, wives, partners and children are the obvious candidates, but there may be other dependents. Suddenly the question of whether this will be a lifestyle or build-to-sell business takes on a new perspective. If you run the business badly and end up with a tax bill that you can't pay, then everyone could suffer.

## 4. What happens if I get ill?

People who run their own businesses can be very exposed if they fall ill. There are hundreds of different types of illness, but they fall into three main types:

1. Unable to work for a short time
2. Unable to work in the same way you used to
3. Unable to work again, ever

Not being able to work for a short while is usually tolerable. It might be a day off with a cold, a week off with a virus, or even two weeks after you have broken a bone or two. But eventually you get back to work, and things are pretty much back to normal. However, if it's any longer than that, then the owner of their own business can really suffer, along with all their dependents. A month out of your own business could put a significant dent in the annual income, three months would take some recovering from, and anything over that could be fatal (to the business, if not you). The second type of illness (not being able to work how you used to) is hugely significant for those whose stock in trade is manual work. If a decorator can't get up a ladder, then he may be deprived of his entire livelihood.

And then there is the extremely nasty third permutation where you can't work again, ever. That's where insurance kicks in. Permanent Health Insurance or an Executive Income Replacement Plan involves paying a monthly premium. If you become incapacitated it will pay you a sensible percentage of your monthly income for the rest of your life if you can't work. This is definitely worth considering if you are the sole breadwinner.

## WHO SAID IT

"Life – how curious is that habit that makes us think it is not here, but elsewhere."
**– V. S. Pritchett**

# WHY PLAN B IS OFTEN BETTER THAN PLAN A

Part of dovetailing a decent lifestyle with the demands of your business involves having reserve plans for every day. When you start running your own business, you may well assume that the shape of tomorrow will be exactly as it is written in your personal organizer. Nothing could be further from the truth. In fact, you should assume every day that everything will change, and become capable of adapting rapidly. You need Plans B, C and so on that you can engage immediately when all the other activities fall away. The trick to avoiding disappointment is to work out that this will happen before it happens. Then when it does, which it undoubtedly will, instead of being aghast at the new development, you simply reach for your Plan B file. Let's have a look at what a Plan B might be, and relish in the thought that the wonderful thing about Plan B is that Plan B is often more productive than Plan A. Here are some examples of things that you can do to generate a Plan B:

1. As a matter of course, you should read all the trade press related to your business, and that which your potential customers read, plus anything else that stimulates you. Collect ideas and articles, and use them to generate initiatives and give you the basis for a speculative phone call or new initiative.

2. If an ex-customer or colleague surfaces some-where in a new job, give them a call and keep an eye out for information on the new market that they have entered. This is how you can extend your customer base beyond its current shape.

3. Have good data sources, become familiar with them, and use them to generate ideas. In par-ticular, remember that trends change all the time, so you need to be on top of developments by checking them regularly.

4. Think of everything that is similar to what you do and consider whether to do that as well. Write down in one sentence precisely what you do for a living and how you make your money. Does the thing that you do or sell have similari-ties with other markets or products? If so, which ones? Could you extend your business into those areas? Does the manner in which you provide a product or service have parallels with other markets? Could you use the same princi-ples to diversify what you do?

If the answer is yes to any of these questions, it does not necessarily mean that you have automatically written the next phase of your business plan. Against any area where you have answered yes, you now need to ask yourself whether you would enjoy doing that particular thing. If the answer is again yes, then you can certainly start to investi-gate the viability of the potential new area. This list is poten-tially endless. The point is that there is always something

# WHO YOU NEED TO KNOW
*Timothy Ferriss*

Timothy Ferriss is an American author, entrepreneur, and public speaker who wrote *The 4-Hour Work Week*, which encouraged people to escape the 9 to 5, live anywhere and join the new rich. His life is a salutary lesson in how to pursue your lifestyle aims and be a business success. Aged 23, Ferriss founded a sports nutrition supplements company which he sold in 2009 to a London-based private equity firm. He is now a full-time angel investor and has invested in many companies including Twitter.

He holds the *Guinness Book of World Records'* record for the most consecutive tango spins in one minute. He and his dance partner Alicia Monti set the record live on television. Before his writing career, Ferriss was the national champion in the 1999 Chinese kickboxing championships. In 2008, he won *Wired Magazine*'s 'Greatest Self-Promoter of All Time' prize and was named one of Fast Company's 'Most Innovative Business People of 2007'.In his show *Trial By Fire* he had one week to learn a skill normally learned over the course of many years and in the pilot episode he practised the Japanese art of horseback archery, Yabusame.

His teachings fit under the umbrella of what he calls lifestyle design, in which he promotes mini-retirements as an alternative to the deferred-life career path where one would work a 9 to 5 job until retirement. This involves breaking what he calls outdated assumptions and finding ways to be more effective so that work takes up less of people's time.

else to investigate. This type of thinking often holds the key to the healthy development of your business.

# TAKE THE ISSUES SERIOUSLY, BUT NOT YOURSELF

So to finish our journey, here is a maxim that really, really works. Customers want their issues taken seriously, but this doesn't mean that you have to do things in a boring way. Earnest subject matter does not mean that the people dealing with it have to be in a permanent state of melancholy. So relax and don't take it *too* seriously. Humour and lightness of touch are great ways of staying calm and sane. A good laugh can really take the pressure off. On the other hand, being downhearted too frequently makes you annoyed with yourself, and you can be sure that it's not much fun for those around you either. This is not to suggest that you wear a revolving bow tie and clown suit to your next meeting. But try some of these ideas for lightening up your day:

- ▶ Take some interesting photos of a hobby or holiday to your next meeting
- ▶ Give a customer a small present such as a box of chocolates
- ▶ Send them an amusing article or quote from the paper
- ▶ Recommend a show, film or album that you think they might like that has absolutely nothing to do with work

You get the idea. These are pleasant and interesting things to do. They are not strictly work, but they will make work more enjoyable for you and your customers. Take the issues seriously, but not yourself. Customers will hugely appreciate it if you do, and it could become the basis of a rewarding blend between your desired lifestyle and business success.

This book is finished, but for you it's just the beginning. It is wise to follow the sequence of work suggested by the chapter order, but if necessary you can dip into specific subjects to unclog those areas that are holding you up. Start by rigorously assessing the nature of your business idea, and generating a really good plan. Apprise yourself of all the legal, technical and financial matters that are important to the smooth running of your business, and then move on to selling and marketing. If relevant, devote plenty of time to designing the team and recruiting the right people, and then you are ready to go. Coping with growth and long-term success is a nice problem to have, so make sure that you balance all the frenetic business activity with a lifestyle that suits you. A diligent approach is likely to reap great rewards. So put the work in and your business will almost certainly be a great success. It's time to get cracking. Good luck.

## WHAT YOU NEED TO READ

▶ Richard Branson's *Screw It Let's Do It* (Virgin Books) is a thoroughly inspirational quick read that explains how it is not only possible but thoroughly desirable to meld your desired lifestyle with the fortunes of the business you run.

► *How To Be Idle* by Tom Hodgkinson (Penguin) provides an alternative take on lifestyle. If business is a means to an end, then it is important to be able to enjoy leisure properly. If you are inclined to become too immersed in work and have difficulty switching off, this book will help.

► *www.seriousplay.com* helps you and your team get to the real issues faster and enhance business performance through a better awareness of commitment and shared goals. This will help you combine lifestyle elements with commercial ones.

► Robert Ashton's *The Life Plan* (Prentice Hall) contains 700 ways to change your life for the better, and attempts to help you balance success and happiness in easy steps.

► *www.theworkfoundation.com* gives a broad range of information on improving the quality of working life and the effectiveness of businesses. It can equip you with evidence, advice, new thinking, networks and events, as well as being an independent authority on work and its future.

▶ *The Play Ethic* by Pat Kane (Pan MacMillan) is a manifesto for a different way of living that explains how play can not only be the antidote to a work-dominated society, but also central to it. In other words, so-called 'play' elements are now fundamental to many businesses. His theory on lifestyle militants is particularly interesting.

# IF YOU ONLY REMEMBER ONE THING

Making your business fit your lifestyle is important for your long-term happiness and the success of your business.

# INDEX

**A**

Accounts  31, 63–65, 68–70,
    79, 85, 86, 90, 103, 190,
    191
attitude  174
Attitude  82, 97, 142, 177,
    180

**B**

Banks  27, 48, 59, 65, 68, 78,
    81, 84–86, 90
Build-to-sell questions  177,
    187
Business  i, 2–5, 8–25, 27–35,
    38, 39, 41–49, 51–58,
    60–62, 64–75, 77–80,
    82–104, 106–119,
    121–127, 129–133,
    136, 137, 141, 142,
    146–156, 158–164,
    166, 167, 169,
    171–175, 178–180,
    182–203
Business plan  3, 38, 42,
    45–47, 51, 53, 57, 59,
    61, 62, 67, 197

**C**

Company culture  177, 179
Contact strategy  105, 116
Customers  3, 7, 13, 16,
    20–22, 24, 25, 30, 33, 35,
    39, 41–43, 45, 47, 52, 53,
    56, 57, 73–76, 92–95, 97,
    99–101, 106, 108, 110,
    112–114, 118, 120, 121,
    123–130, 132, 146, 152,
    153, 160, 161, 166, 168,
    171, 173, 184, 185, 188,
    192, 193, 196, 199, 200
Customer insights  100, 110,
    116, 174, 186

**D**

Describing what you do 38, 105, 123

Durability 158, 170, 172, 173, 175, 185

**E**

Execution 7, 25, 28

**F**

Finance 62, 68, 81, 84, 88–90, 103

**G**

Getting help you need 5, 17, 29, 33, 48, 52–55, 57, 68, 70, 72, 74, 83, 86, 101, 112, 119, 127, 138, 145, 158, 160, 180

Growth 71, 122, 157–161, 169, 170, 173–175, 201

**I**

Idea 2, 4, 10–13, 15, 17, 19–23, 25–28, 31–35, 38, 39, 54, 59, 67, 68, 74, 89, 91, 96–98, 100, 110–115, 120, 121, 126, 127, 132, 138, 141–144, 146, 153, 156, 163, 173, 174, 182, 184, 196, 197, 200, 201

Insurance 63, 67, 77, 78, 91, 195

Investment 48, 53, 61, 88, 89, 107, 150, 172, 192

Issues 28, 60, 74, 106, 110, 120, 121, 136, 145, 146, 148, 149, 155, 159, 163, 172, 175, 177, 199, 200, 202

**L**

Laws 3, 64, 66–68, 79, 80, 91, 118, 131

Legal requirements 63, 64, 67, 72, 77, 78

Lifestyle 136, 177, 178, 187, 192–194, 196, 198–203

Lifestyle questions 136, 142, 145, 153, 156, 161, 163, 167, 173, 177–180, 185, 187, 188, 192–194, 196–203

Looking ahead 81, 99

**M**

Margin 16, 18, 24, 45, 50, 51, 73, 81, 82, 86, 92, 94, 96, 101, 102, 104, 111, 119, 159, 160

Marketing i, 3, 14, 56, 73, 74, 76, 93, 94, 99, 105–111, 113–116, 119, 120, 122–126, 128, 130, 133, 201

Meetings 67, 105, 117, 121, 130–132, 148, 154, 166

Money 3, 7, 9, 10, 23, 25, 30, 37–39, 41, 48, 49, 53, 54, 57, 58, 60, 65, 66, 70, 82–90, 92, 95, 96, 99,

101, 102, 104, 108, 127,
132, 136, 154, 160, 172,
189, 190, 191, 197
Motivation 3, 9, 51, 89

**N**
Name and identity 55
Networking 105, 130, 131

**O**
One-page business plan 41
Online marketing 105, 128

**P**
Pay 10, 24, 25, 29, 45, 49,
64–66, 73, 77, 81, 86,
90–94, 99, 103, 108, 112,
127, 139, 144, 148, 172,
181, 194, 195
People 2, 3, 8, 13, 14, 19,
22–24, 28, 30, 31, 38, 49,
52, 60, 66, 74, 75, 82,
93, 94, 99, 106, 108,
110–113, 117, 118,
120–123, 126, 129–132,
134–137, 139, 140, 142,
146–156, 159, 163, 164,
166, 169, 171, 179, 186,
188, 191, 192, 194, 198,
199–201
Personal style 146, 180, 186
Plan B 177, 196
Plans 2, 7, 18–20, 23, 25,
27–29, 38, 59, 67, 73, 74,
77, 79, 84, 85, 89, 91,
109–111, 128, 177, 182,

192, 193, 195, 196, 201,
202
Pre-marketing 111, 116
Problems 13, 17, 27, 70, 89,
100, 102, 106, 111, 135,
143–146, 155, 160, 172,
188
Product 8, 13, 14, 16, 18–26,
32, 33, 35, 53, 55, 56,
61, 67, 68, 74, 76, 78,
82, 83, 85, 90–93, 95,
99–104, 106, 107,
110–113, 118, 120–124,
126, 127, 129, 144, 148,
157, 160, 161, 163, 185,
197
Product analysis
Keeping things varied 157,
166
Rewarding yourself 183
Services 8, 13, 16, 18–25,
32, 33, 60, 67, 74, 83,
85, 92–94, 99, 107, 110,
112–114, 117, 118, 121,
127, 132, 157, 161, 163,
185
Progress not perfection 53
Proposition 12, 21, 32,
37–39, 61, 77, 78, 125

**R**
Recruiting 135, 140, 201
Researching your market 7,
60
Reviews 25, 28, 74, 79, 99,
100, 102, 119, 128, 163

**S**

Sales 3, 16, 26, 73, 76, 82–84, 86, 88, 95, 100, 104, 105, 107, 109, 111, 123, 127, 129–131, 159, 165

Self-belief 29, 30

Services 144

Setbacks 157, 171

Starting 2–5, 8–10, 13–15, 17, 19, 20, 22, 24, 25, 28, 30, 33, 34, 38, 46, 53, 58, 61, 62, 64, 67, 69, 77, 79, 80, 82, 88, 94, 97, 100, 103, 104, 109, 115, 136, 147, 158, 187

Staying in touch 73, 84, 152

Sustaining relationships 135, 147

Systems 3, 29, 30, 43, 63, 64, 68–70, 72–76, 79, 80, 82, 84–86, 117, 119, 120, 168, 172

**T**

Tax 64–66, 69, 70, 78, 79, 81, 85, 86, 90, 91, 103, 181, 190, 194

Teams 151, 171

Technology 31, 63, 70, 79, 141

Test-driving 32

**W**

What do *you* want 8

Working environment 38, 51, 52, 61